Cambridge Elements

Elements in Language, Gender and Sexuality
edited by
Helen Sauntson
York St John University

LINGUISTIC REPRESENTATIONS OF WOMEN IN OLD ENGLISH PROSE

A Corpus-Based Phraseological Study

Anna Cichosz
University of Lodz

Tomasz Dobrogoszcz
University of Lodz

Shaftesbury Road, Cambridge CB2 8EA, United Kingdom

One Liberty Plaza, 20th Floor, New York, NY 10006, USA

477 Williamstown Road, Port Melbourne, VIC 3207, Australia

314–321, 3rd Floor, Plot 3, Splendor Forum, Jasola District Centre, New Delhi – 110025, India

103 Penang Road, #05–06/07, Visioncrest Commercial, Singapore 238467

Cambridge University Press is part of Cambridge University Press & Assessment, a department of the University of Cambridge.

We share the University's mission to contribute to society through the pursuit of education, learning and research at the highest international levels of excellence.

www.cambridge.org
Information on this title: www.cambridge.org/9781009625807
DOI: 10.1017/9781009625791

© Anna Cichosz and Tomasz Dobrogoszcz 2025

This publication is in copyright. Subject to statutory exception and to the provisions of relevant collective licensing agreements, with the exception of the Creative Commons version the link for which is provided below, no reproduction of any part may take place without the written permission of Cambridge University Press & Assessment.

An online version of this work is published at doi.org/10.1017/9781009625791 under a Creative Commons Open Access license CC-BY-NC 4.0 which permits re-use, distribution and reproduction in any medium for non-commercial purposes providing appropriate credit to the original work is given and any changes made are indicated. To view a copy of this license visit https://creativecommons.org/licenses/by-nc/4.0

When citing this work, please include a reference to the DOI 10.1017/9781009625791

First published 2025

A catalogue record for this publication is available from the British Library

ISBN 978-1-009-62580-7 Hardback
ISBN 978-1-009-62576-0 Paperback
ISSN 2634-8772 (online)
ISSN 2634-8764 (print)

Cambridge University Press & Assessment has no responsibility for the persistence or accuracy of URLs for external or third-party internet websites referred to in this publication and does not guarantee that any content on such websites is, or will remain, accurate or appropriate.

For EU product safety concerns, contact us at Calle de José Abascal, 56, 1°, 28003 Madrid, Spain, or email eugpsr@cambridge.org

Linguistic Representations of Women in Old English Prose

A Corpus-Based Phraseological Study

Elements in Language, Gender and Sexuality

DOI: 10.1017/9781009625791
First published online: December 2025

Anna Cichosz
University of Lodz

Tomasz Dobrogoszcz
University of Lodz

Author for correspondence: Anna Cichosz, anna.cichosz@uni.lodz.pl

Abstract: This Element traces the origins and earliest manifestations of gender bias in the English language. The analysis is based on a corpus of Old English prose texts, written between the ninth and the eleventh centuries. The results are interpreted in the historical, cultural and literary context of Anglo-Saxon England and early medieval Europe. The investigation shows a significant difference in the way women and men are presented in Old English texts, with the former clearly associated with family life, portrayed in the context of their physical appearance, marriage and childbearing, rarely involved in meaningful activities and presented as possessions of their male relatives. Situating the linguistic representations of women in the context of Christianity, the Element demonstrates that late Old English can be seen as a vehicle of language bias that will establish male domination for centuries to come. This title is also available as Open Access on Cambridge Core.

Keywords: Old English, gender bias, phraseology, corpus study, feminism, Anglo-Saxon women

© Anna Cichosz and Tomasz Dobrogoszcz 2025

ISBNs: 9781009625807 (HB), 9781009625760 (PB), 9781009625791 (OC)
ISSNs: 2634-8772 (online), 2634-8764 (print)

Contents

Introduction   1

1 Old English Written Records and Linguistic Insights into Anglo-Saxon Culture   2

2 Language and Gender   8

3 Collocations on the Level of the Noun Phrase   18

4 Collocations on the Level of the Verb Phrase   63

Conclusions   90

References   94

Introduction

When Luce Irigaray considers the differences between women's and men's discourses, she draws attention to the historicality of social communication practices: 'Language is a product of the sedimentations of languages of former eras. Every era has its specific needs, creates its own ideals, and imposes them as such. Some are more historically durable than others: sexual ideals are a good example here. These ideals have gradually imposed their norms on our language' (Irigaray, 1993: 30).

Examining 'cultural injustices' and 'generalized sexism' manifested in language, she notes that positive valuation of the masculine and negative appraisal of the feminine has been a linguistic condition lasting for centuries (Irigaray, 1993: 68). It is only natural, then, that feminist interrogations of language as a tool of discrimination will look both into the present and into the past, encroaching on the territory traditionally ascribed to sociolinguistics and historical linguistics, bringing new insights and a fresh perspective on linguistic data.

Sociolinguistics has analysed the relation between gender and language from two research perspectives. On the one hand, numerous studies have focused on the analysis of the way in which women and men differ in their *use of language* (including, e.g., Lakoff, 1975; Spender, 1980; Fishman, 1983). On the other hand, many other scholars have investigated the way in which men and women are *represented in language*, which led to the coinage of the term *linguistic sexism* (Pauwels, 2005). Despite its patent advantages, the former perspective cannot be applied to a great number of historical texts, since female authors are practically absent from medieval records of any European language, including English. As a result, scholars quite unanimously admit that 'there might not be much material to throw light on matters such as social gender differences in Old English' (Nevalainen & Raumolin-Brunberg, 2014: 18), since:

> [t]he texts we do have are all the result of a tiny literate proportion of society – we can have no idea of how the average farm worker or travelling merchant spoke. Such persons remain, forever, a hidden majority. The literate community, furthermore, were, for the most part, members of religious communities, and this necessarily further limits the type of language which was written down. Those who wrote down our texts, although not necessarily those who composed the thoughts that were written down, were from a highly restricted stratum of the society. They were also likely to be from only a restricted age group, and virtually none of them were female. (Hogg, 2006: 395)

Therefore, even though Anglo-Saxon textual records are relatively rich, the impact of social variables such as gender, age, education or social class on the

English language may be analysed only from the early modern period onwards (Nevalainen & Raumolin-Brunberg, 2014), because in the sixteenth century a growing number of English-speaking women became literate and started to produce private correspondence.[1] Nevertheless, even for earlier stages of English it is technically possible to analyse the way in which women and men are represented in historical texts. So far, there have been no comprehensive corpus-based diachronic studies of this topic in the context of English, which means that it is still not clear how the linguistic image of men and women has evolved over the centuries. The aim of this Element is to fill in this gap and take a closer look at gender representation in the earliest records of English by means of advanced corpus methods, interpreting the results in a larger framework of feminist theory.

Considering the historical origins of the disadvantaged socio-cultural position of women, Cixous (1976: 876) argues that they were 'led into self-disdain by the great arm of parental-conjugal phallocentrism' which was 'self-admiring, self-stimulating [and] self-congratulatory' (879), and manifested also in the power of discourse. If, as feminist linguists claim, gender-based oppression is and has been orchestrated through language, it seems particularly rewarding to trace this oppression back to early medieval times, to the stereotypical representations of gender differences which this Element attempts to demonstrate in the context of the English language. These representations contributed to the formulation of linguistic identity of women and men, informing English-speaking culture for subsequent centuries and legitimising its gender bias. Irigaray (1993: 31) identifies gender bias in language as an effect of an intentional strategy: 'Man seems to have wanted, directly or indirectly, to give the universe his own gender as he has wanted to give his own name to his children, his wife, his possessions.'

1 Old English Written Records and Linguistic Insights into Anglo-Saxon Culture

Old English (OE) is a very well-attested early medieval language: the total length of all surviving texts written by Anglo-Saxons in their vernacular amounts to the impressive figure of 3 million words. This calculation includes poetry, interlinear glosses from Latin and prose texts, many of which have been preserved in multiple copies. The York–Toronto–Helsinki Parsed Corpus of Old English Prose (YCOE, Taylor et al., 2003) includes texts which cover

---

[1] Wormald (1977: 113) describes the early medieval situation of the Anglo-Saxon community as 'a clerical monopoly', with few literate lay (male) individuals, and by the end of the Middle English period the picture had not changed substantially, since 'in 1500 an aggregate of perhaps 5 per cent of adult males and 1 per cent of adult females could sign their names in England' (Fox, 2000: 18).

1.5 million words, omitting textual overlaps and word-for-word glosses of questionable value for syntactic investigations. The number might not be impressive from a contemporary corpus perspective, but for a historical language it is a considerable amount of data, allowing for the formulation of reliable conclusions based on recurrent patterns. Therefore, OE is a very good choice for a historical linguist wishing to study the earliest stage of development of an Indo-European language, and it provides a unique opportunity to analyse the relations between culture and language in the early medieval European context.

Naturally, our knowledge of Anglo-Saxon literary culture is mostly based on the well-known Germanic poetry records, including, for example, *Beowulf*, *The Wanderer*, *The Seafarer* and *The Dream of the Rood*. These works, however, famous as they are, constitute a really small portion of OE textual records. The York–Helsinki Parsed Corpus of Old English Poetry (Pintzuk & Plug, 2001) includes only 71,490 words in total, which is a significantly lower number than the 1.5 million words of the YCOE. What is more, the texts included in the prose corpus, even though most of them are fully focused on the Catholic faith, are quite varied in character. The most frequent genres are homilies (390,925 words altogether), lives of saints (298,316 words), chronicles (236,165 words), biblical translations (136,948 words), religious treatises (129,993 words) and medical remedies (68,315 words), while some minor text types include law collections, prefaces, travelogues, charters and wills. Thus the analysis of OE prose records may provide much more insight into the linguistic reality of Anglo-Saxon England than the study of poetic records, not only because of the sheer quantity of the data, but also because prose works, which are predominantly non-literary texts, may reflect a more conventionalised linguistic image of women in Anglo-Saxon society. Since literary language, which aspires to produce an aesthetic effect rather than conveying straightforward information, avoids patterns and regularities, the analysis of non-literary prose records might yield linguistic evidence with more reality value.

It is only predictable that written historical sources from the Anglo-Saxon period – chronicles, ecclesiastical documents, legal codes or wills – focus chiefly on the male part of society, making women significantly absent. Moreover, the civilisation reflected in Anglo-Saxon poetry was co-ordinated by tribal warfare and naturally centred on men, who formed the warrior class, while women could only assume 'the non-roles of . . . peaceweaver and mourner for the dead' or become symbolic treasure facilitating political goals (Bennett, 1994: 43–45). Many marriages of the epoch were arranged, particularly but not solely in aristocratic circles; Anglo-Saxon women were 'linked to male kin-groups' and matrimony meant exchanging the custody of one man for 'a new role of submission to another' (Leyser, 1995: 47). The gendered division of population demanded that female activity concentrate on the family and local community matters, not public spheres. The division of labour in the peasant class also depended on sex: heavy agricultural work and craftsmanship was the males' responsibility, while women engaged in 'a wide variety of smaller tasks centered on the household' (Bennett, 1988: 18). Fell (1986: 40) notes that early Anglo-Saxon culture 'distinguished male and female roles as those of the warrior or hunter and of the cloth-maker'. Indeed, archaeological evidence reveals that women were often buried with thread boxes, needles, spindle whorls, table linen or other pieces of cloth (Fell, 1986: 40–44; Leyser, 1995: 3–15); their burial places also indicate involvement in other domestic activities, such as the preparation and the serving of food and drink (Fell, 1986: 47–49) or medical assistance (Leyser, 1995: 15).

Examining the position of women in Anglo-Saxon society is especially problematic because the scholarly tradition that dominated the field until the 1990s continuously concealed the female presence from the study of historical reality, leaving 'no place for a woman scholar who wanted to read as a woman' (Bennett, 1994: 43). Norris et al. (2023: 10) explain these discriminating patriarchal academic paradigms with the fact that the field of early medieval English studies was established 'at the height of British imperialism', and it developed in a political environment which 'supported claims to White, male, European superiority'. Lees (1997: 148) also claims that 'the institutional structures of the discipline' have persistently marginalised 'the role of women in the formation of [Anglo-Saxon] culture'. Desmond in turn notes that standard literary history studies (such as Greenfield's 1965 *A Critical History of Old English Literature*), rooted in masculine ideology and purporting neutral objectivity, fail to notice the 'tremendous importance of women in Anglo-Saxon culture, as authors, characters, or voices' (Desmond, 1990: 575).

As in other fields of cultural and literary studies, feminist criticism attempts to redefine the framework of scholarly approaches to OE texts: it challenges masculinist biased presuppositions, reconsiders the omissions of patriarchal paradigms of historical inquiry, retrieves silenced women's voices and reclaims suppressed women's perspectives. Early feminist studies of Anglo-Saxon literature, by such authors as Anne Klinck and Elaine Tuttle Hansen, already in the late 1970s examined OE poetry with the view of situating female anguish, confinement and submission in the context of early medieval English culture as well as moral implications of its poetic representation (Overing, 1990: 76–77). Yet a wave of a more determined feminist response rose in the mid 1980s with the publications of Christine E. Fell, Jane Chance and Helen Damico, who strived to recognise women's position in Anglo-Saxon society by means of presenting notable female individuals – queens, aristocrats, saints, abbesses – 'to advance the argument that Anglo-Saxon society was relatively ... egalitarian' and to establish the 'so-called "golden age" for Anglo-Saxon women' (Lees, 1997: 148–149). In her monumental 1984 work *Women in Anglo-Saxon England*, Fell, a historian, inspects multiple records of the epoch – vernacular literature, hagiography, legal documents, letters, inventories, archaeological evidence – to demonstrate the position and agency of women in early medieval English culture. In her study published two years later, *Woman as Hero in Old English Literature*, Chance (1986: 111) contradicts Fell's confident view of female significance, pointing out that 'Anglo-Saxon society demanded passivity, rather than leadership and initiative, from most of its women.' The scholar finds 'exceptions' (111) of strong female individuals but notes that they were 'permitted an active political role in kingdoms as chaste rulers or strong abbesses, and some became saints who were even allowed to adopt heroic behavior ... once their chastity and sanctity had been attested' (xv): that is to say, 'the escape from passivity may only be accomplished by ... an obliteration of femininity ... women may be not-weak as long as they are not-women' (Overing, 1990: 78). Damico (1984) in turn seeks to subvert the pattern of female passivity in early medieval England by re-examining one of the most eminent examples of Old English poetic discourse, *Beowulf*, to interpret Queen Wealhtheow as 'an autonomously powerful military figure, with the additional mythic and distinctively menacing qualities of the valkyrie' (Bennett et al., 1990: 17).

Since the 1990s, feminist studies of Anglo-Saxon culture have continued with a rising awareness that gender actively interrelates to other aspects of human identity and cannot be reviewed in isolation. Recent feminist approaches to the field show an interesting dichotomy. On the one hand, a number of scholars endeavour to evidence substantial marginalisation and objectification of women in early medieval England. Overing (1990: 69–70), for instance, finds *Beowulf* 'an overwhelmingly masculine poem' which does not provide any place for women 'in [its] masculine economy': she believes that the Anglo-Saxon 'system of masculine alliance allows women to signify [only] in a system of apparent exchange', but not 'in their own right' (74), leaving them 'profoundly silent' (70) and 'excluded figures' (75). Similarly, Fee (1996: 290) discerns in *Beowulf*'s parallel between the rituals of ring-giving and peace-weaving the analogy which 'exists between objects of material treasure and objectified women in the culture of the poem': according to the transactional nature of Anglo-Saxon marriage, women 'serve as commodities which are exchanged in order to safeguard a particular social or political agenda' (285). On the other hand, there are concurrent approaches which intend to reclaim female agency in early medieval England and demonstrate that in the texts of this period 'women are often depicted in roles which ... are invested with more importance and capability' than later (Harris, 2014). This agency could be visible in their discourse, like Wealhtheow's speeches, which, for Damico (2015: 206), prove her authority as 'a female sovereign central to the administrative power of the court'. Alternatively, it could be part of other activities: for instance, Lee (2023: 53) discerns it in their production of embroidery, 'artifacts that provide a unique window to the participation ... in the political, socio-economic, and intellectual life of the period'.

The relatively privileged status of women in Anglo-Saxon society was postulated and amply illustrated by Fell. The historian refers to numerous legal documents which testify to measures meant to protect women's standing. Among them, there is *morgengifu*, 'morning-gift', the money that the prospective husband had to pay to effectuate marriage; importantly, it was 'paid not to the father or kin, but to the woman herself', and she could fully control it, for example, spend it, give it away, or bequeath it (Fell, 1986: 56), because finances in marriage were 'held to be the property of husband and wife, not of husband only' (57). Fell also points to legal provisions regarding the economic status of widows or the protection of women against seduction and rape. She evokes instances of wills written by women or those in which men left property to their wives, mothers or daughters. Archaeological evidence or place names originated in this period also attest to women's financial independence. Fell's findings, as well as other related publications, indicate that even though women were not equal to men in terms of their legal and economic status, they 'enjoyed a significant degree of autonomy' (Desmond 1990: 585).

Yet Fell (1986: 14) discerns a 'complete shift of pattern ... within a single century after 1066': the status of women in medieval England became aggravated after the Norman Conquest. This observation follows the postulate of Doris Stenton from her long-recognised work *The English Woman in History*: '[W]omen [in Anglo-Saxon England] were ... more nearly the equal companions of their husbands and brothers than at any other period before the modern age. In the higher ranges of society this rough and ready partnership was ended by the Norman Conquest, which introduced into England a military society relegating women to a position honourable but essentially unimportant' (Stenton, 1957: 348). This decline of female position could be seen, for instance, in economical rights: Anglo-Norman women could no longer hold land and make wills independently (Fell, 1986: 154; Leyser, 1995: 74). Many historians interpret this as a result of changes in the inheritance system, which became based on male primogeniture (Fell, 1986: 149; Leyser, 1995: 83). It was also, however, related to a modified approach to the feudal system: if in post-Conquest England 'all land belonged to the king, ... its use was conditional on the performance of military service' and therefore 'only men could hold land' (Leyser, 1995: 86).

This conventional argument about the post-Conquest radical shift in the situation of women in England has been an object of criticism. Anne L. Klinck (1982: 109), for instance, argues that 'there is a much closer resemblance between the situation obtaining in late Anglo-Saxon England and post-Conquest England than there is between the early and late Anglo-Saxon period' and, therefore, 'to describe Anglo-Saxon England as a time when women enjoyed an independence which they lost as a result of changes introduced by the Norman Conquest is misleading'. Many feminist scholars claim that what really brought the change was the growing socio-cultural influence of Christianity and, especially, the institutional dimension of the church. Fell herself notes that 'Christianity as interpreted by the fathers of the church developed a full set of theories on the inferiority of women', but she puts into doubt 'the extent of their actual application within society' (Fell, 1986: 13): even though she admits that we can easily find 'traces of anti-female propaganda in letters or homilies from the pens of clergy and in the penitentials', she authoritatively deems them 'ineffectual in practice' (13–14). For Chance (1986: xvii), however, the significance of the church should not be underestimated: she notes that the 'two archetypes of women that ordered the Anglo-Saxon social world' – Eve and the Virgin Mary – were of obvious religious roots, 'drawn from the Bible'. In her later work, Chance openly asserts that women in medieval England, just like in any other European country of the era, 'were always propelled by the misogyny of the church, and a masculine church at that' (Chance, 2007: 7). Perhaps the most persuasive work demonstrating the impact of the church on the degradation of the female position in late Anglo-Saxon society is Stephanie Hollis' *Anglo-Saxon Women and the Church*. The scholar postulates that the deterioration of the standing of women, especially monastic women, dates 'from at least as early as the 8th century' (Hollis, 1992: 7), and that from Alfred's reign 'the literature reveals an increase in the prestige and authority of male ecclesiastics and a reduction in the status of women [which] parallels the overall tendency of canon law' (1). Hollis strongly opposes Fell's downplaying of 'the social actualization of the church's heritage of doctrines inimical to women' (7) and points out it is impossible to deny 'the social dominance of an institution whose most committed members were responsible for the composition and preservation of the only written evidence available to us' (6). She sees this actualisation in numerous Anglo-Saxon texts, for instance in Bede's hagiography, which propagates the opinion that 'women constitute a separate and inferior class' (8), or in Theodore's penitential canons, which represent numerous 'repressive conceptions of women ... harboured by at least some churchmen, which fairly certainly included the most influential of them' (8). The critic sees the conversion of England as a long process of cultural negotiation in which '[p]atristic-derived conceptions of women, ... through mapping on to indigenous prejudices and inequalities, established themselves only slowly in Anglo-Saxon England' (10) and contends that, at the end of the day, 'what the assimilation of Roman-Christianity achieved was the alterization of women' (10). This process must have been reflected in language and therefore, given the historical context, it seems both logical and necessary to take a look at the OE prose records, which are dominated by religious texts, in order to investigate the influence of Roman Christianity on the linguistic image of Anglo-Saxon women.

2 Language and Gender

Feminists have always considered language an important territory of their emancipatory struggle. Yet the onset of substantial and systematic research in feminist linguistics started only in the 1970s and 1980s. One of the landmark publications was Robin Lakoff's *Language and Woman's Place* (1975), which, by means of depicting 'a culture-wide ideology that scorns and trivializes both women and women's ways of speaking' (Bucholtz, 2014: 26), revealed the political capacity of language to devalue and disempower women. An even more radical approach is pursued by Dale Spender in *Man Made Language* (1980). A wholehearted proponent of the Sapir–Whorf hypothesis, Spender notes that 'it is language which determines the limits of our world [and] constructs our reality' (Spender, 1980: 139), so that this reality is determined by its linguistic representation. Naturally, then, those who control language are especially privileged, as they also control our notion of reality; Spender claims that men are the superior class which 'has controlled language in its own interest, constructing sexist categories and meanings through which all speakers of the language view the world' (Hendricks & Oliver, 1999). In her very comprehensive study of the intersections between feminism and linguistics, *Feminism and Linguistic Theory* (1992), Deborah Cameron points out that in the view of radical feminist theorists 'male language is a species of Orwellian thought-control' (Cameron, 1992: 129); if, as they believe, 'words embody sexism because their meaning and usage is fixed by men from an antifeminist perspective', then language can be considered 'a cause of oppression, and not just a symptom of it' (104).[2] Cameron emphasises the indebtedness of many

---

[2] Cameron distinguishes between two general explanations of linguistic sexism: for some feminists, sexist language is a 'symptom', an unintentional manifestation of the unfavourable perception of women by culture; for others, it is a 'cause', a calculated element of masculinist ideology (Cameron, 1992: 101–104).

feminist linguists to the theory of Jacques Lacan, who postulates that human subjectivity is formed through being introduced to the symbolic order of language. In this way, the roots of our identity reach the past generations because 'language, with its structure, exists prior to each subject's entry into it at a certain moment in [their] mental development' (Lacan, 2006: 413). The French psychoanalyst also notes the patriarchal nature of the symbolic order, claiming that '[i]t is in the *name of the father* that we must recognize the basis of the symbolic function which, since the dawn of historical time, has identified his person with the figure of the law' (230). This has obvious political consequences which feminist linguists have pointed out: 'inserting oneself into culture means submitting to patriarchy' (Cameron, 1992: 169).

Whether or not feminist linguists advocate the Sapir–Whorf theory and Lacan's position, they mostly agree that language is a gendered phenomenon and that its ideologies inform our socio-political reality. They also concur that linguistic representations of men and women can function as

> part of a society's apparatus for maintaining gender distinctions and hierarchies. At the most basic level, they help to naturalize the notion of the sexes as 'opposite', with differing natures and social roles or responsibilities. Often, too, they naturalize the social inequalities which are associated with gender difference. [Some] feminine qualities are readily invoked to explain and justify the exclusion or marginalization of women in powerful or public roles, while at the same time reinforcing the idea of their natural suitability for other, more menial, tasks. ... Ideological representations do not in and of themselves accomplish the subordination of women. *Their contribution is rather to justify inequality, making the relationship of women and men in a particular society appear natural and legitimate rather than arbitrary and unfair.* (Cameron, 2014: 285, emphasis ours)

Sexist bias is a very complex mechanism manifested on many different levels of language organisation. Feminist linguists indicate that 'the lexicon and grammatical system of English contains features that exclude, insult and trivialise women' (Cameron, 1992: 101).[3] As Weatherall (2002: 13) notes, linguistic manifestations of sexism may roughly be divided into three categories: 'language that ignores women; language that defines women narrowly; and language that depreciates women'.

One of the most conspicuous issues raised by feminists, clearly related to Weatherall's (2002) 'ignoring' type, is 'the practice of considering the man/the

---

[3] Linguistic sexism is a phenomenon which has been observed and described not only in English, but also for a wide variety of languages (cf. Blakar 1977 and Uri 2018 for Norwegian, Irigaray 1985 and 1993 as well as Yaguello 1978 for French, Guentherodt et al. 1980 for German, García Meseguer 1977 for Spanish, Karwatowska & Szpyra-Kozłowska 2005 for Polish, etc.).

male as the prototype for human representation' (Pauwels, 2005: 553). This is related to the use of *he* and other masculine generics such as 'chairman', 'mankind', 'guys' or 'fireman' (Weatherall, 2002: 14), the fact that the terms for human and male are often the same (cf. English *man*, whose sense 1 in the Oxford English Dictionary is defined as 'a human being (irrespective of sex or age)') or the frequently derivative nature of female terms (e.g. according to *Etymoline* the English term *woman* is an alternation of the compound *wifmann*, composed of *wif* 'woman, wife' and *man* 'man, human being'). What is more, the occupational titles for women are rarely morphologically marked (with *actress* as a rare exception), and in English it is much more common to mark gender overtly for women (*female doctor*) than for men (*male secretary*) (Marco, 1997), though English is now adopting a corrective strategy of making terms neutral or unmarked for gender, unlike, for example, French or Polish, where the terms are overtly marked as gender specific (Weatherall, 2002: 17), for instance, French *la ministre* or Polish *ministra* as the overtly female equivalent of *minister*.

Another aspect of this problem, fitting Weatherall's (2002) 'narrowing' type, is that women are often (or at least more often than men) discussed in terms of their physical appearance and family relationships, while in the case of men the focus is rather on their profession (Key, 1975). A related issue is the European practice of taking the husband's name after getting married, the fact that female titles, unlike male ones, used to reveal the woman's marital status (Miss and Mrs vs. the more recent, neutral Ms), and the tendency for female nicknames to be based on appearance and often (though not always) show connotations of beauty (e.g. Blondie, Sweetie, Midget), while male nicknames are rather based on activity and show connotations of power and hardness (e.g. Chaser, Mad Dog) (Phillips, 1990; Weatherall, 2002: 23). Finally, within the 'depreciating' type of language sexism, there is a tendency of masculine terms to have more positive connotations than their feminine equivalents (cf. *bachelor* vs. *spinster* or *mister* vs. *mistress*), which results from the fact that with time female terms tend to undergo semantic derogation (Schultz, 1975), changing from once neutral to abusive, 'ending as a sexual slur' (Pauwels, 2005: 554).

Obviously, all of these linguistic aspects of the problem are a logical and clear result of the long-lasting patriarchal structure of European societies, with women's roles limited to those of mothers, wives and lovers, fully dependent on men and often selected and judged on the basis of their physical appearance. The picture is changing right now, and the growing awareness of gender bias in English-language communities is a fact (Pauwels, 2005: 561). The aim of this Element is to take a step back, get to the roots of the issue and investigate the problem of gender representation in the earliest records of English in order to determine how gender bias operated in the Anglo-Saxon reality.

Our initial hypothesis was that at least some of the tendencies which feminist linguists observed in the English language in the 1970s and 1980s should already be visible in the OE data, and many of them should also be identifiable on the basis of recurrent collocations – that is, the fixed combinations of two lexemes that this Element is about to analyse. Therefore, the Element examines to what extent the most frequent collocations centred around a number of gendered nouns reflect the position of women in the Anglo-Saxon society. Our investigation seeks the ways in which OE phraseology suggests a marked difference in the social roles of Anglo-Saxon men and women. Drawing from other sources, we assumed at the outset that linguistic data should show connotations of power, hardness and activity for men, as opposed to beauty, physicality and sexuality for women. We expected that the collocations based on female terms would be more often associated with family relationships and physical appearance, while the equivalent male terms would rather collocate with lexemes focusing on profession or signalling domination. We also believe that establishing which of Weatherall's types of linguistic manifestations of sexism (ignoring, narrowing and depreciating) may be revealed by a corpus-based analysis of collocations should become useful in the operationalisation of linguistic sexism for various language studies.

For the purpose of the Element, in order to analyse the linguistic image of women in OE, it was necessary to preselect a number of women terms and their male equivalents. The procedure was as follows: first, *A Thesaurus of Old English* (Roberts et al., 2000) was browsed in search of all female-gendered nouns attested in this language. Next, the frequency of these words was checked in the VARIOE morphological dictionary for YCOE (Cichosz et al., 2022), and the words were arranged according to their frequency (cf. Table 1).

The list of women terms which we checked was much longer, but it turned out that many of the words included in the thesaurus are limited to poetry records or texts not included in YCOE since they are not attested in the corpus. Table 2 presents these items.

The only women terms from Table 2 which are potentially present in YCOE for which it is impossible to check it automatically because of their morphological overlap with the equivalent men terms are *witege* 'prophetess' (overlapping with *witega* 'prophet') and *widuwe* 'widow' (overlapping with *widuwa* 'widower'). What is more, the primary sense of the word *laf* is 'what is left', and only the secondary meaning is 'widow (f)'. Since it would be impossible to tell the difference without manual inspection in context, the word was discarded. Finally, despite its high frequency, the word *mægþ* had to be eliminated from the dataset since its secondary sense – that is, 'family' – turned out to be dominant in the data and the lexeme failed to appear in collocations reflecting its primary sense 'maiden, girl'.

Table 1 Women terms from *A Thesaurus of Old English* with their YCOE frequency

Old English word	Sense	Corpus frequency
wif	female person/woman; wife/married woman	1,404
modor	mother; abbess	530
mægden	girl; maiden; female servant	430
dohtor	daughter	380
mægþ	maiden; girl	373
fæmne	female person/woman; female child; maiden	313
sweostor	sister; nun	190
cwen	female person/woman; wife/married woman; queen; noble lady	172
wifmann	female person/woman; female servant	118
abbodesse	abbess	69
hlæfdige	abbess; queen; noble lady; lady	60
nunne	nun	52
bryd	wife/married woman; bride	39
wiln	handmaid, woman slave	31
gesweostor	sisters	29
mynecenu	nun	27
wicce	witch/sorceress	22
gyden	goddess	18
modrige	aunt	15
cennestre	mother	14
sweger	mother-in-law	14
snoru	daughter-in-law	11
rihtæw	rightful wife	8
gesiþwif	noble lady	7
cifes	concubine/harlot	7
mægdencild	female child	7
faþu	aunt	6
steopmodor	stepmother	5
domne	abbess; lady	4
forlegis	harlot/whore/adulteress	3
witegestre	prophetess	3
ælæte	divorced woman	2
broþorwif	sister-in-law	2
dryicge	witch/sorceress	2
duruþinen	female doorkeeper	2

Table 1 (cont.)

Old English word	Sense	Corpus frequency
festermodor	foster-mother	2
forlegiswif	harlot/whore/adulteress	2
goddohtor	god-daughter	2
hægtesse	witch/sorceress; enchantress	2
horcwene	harlot/whore/adulteress	2
leodrune	enchantress	2
nefne	niece	2
rihtwif	rightful wife	2
casern	queen/empress	1
forligerwif	prostitute	1
gedohtra	daughters	1
godmodor	godmother	1
hoppestre	female dancer	1
mynsterfæmne	nun	1
nift	granddaughter; niece; stepdaughter	1
scericge	female jester	1
sealticge	female dancer	1
þeowe	female servant; woman slave	1
wælcyrge	witch/sorceress	1
wifcild	female child	1

Table 2 Women terms from *A Thesaurus of Old English* not attested in YCOE

Old English word	Translation	Old English word	Translation
acennicge	mother	*ides*	female person/woman
æwe	wife/married woman	*laf*	widow; what is left
bearncennicge	mother	*locbore*	free woman
bepæcestre	harlot/whore/adulteress	*lufestre*	harlot/whore/adulteress
burgrun(e)	enchantress	*lybbestre*	witch/sorceress
byrþre	mother	*lytle*	woman slave
cumendre	godmother	*mennen*	handmaiden
cummædre	godmother	*meowle*	female person/woman; maiden

Table 2 (cont.)

Old English word	Translation	Old English word	Translation
dryhtcwen	queen/empress	myltestre	prostitute
duruþeowen	female doorkeeper	nefe	granddaughter
ealdre	abbess	nunfæmne	nun
ealdwif	old woman	nydhæmestre	harlot/whore/adulteress
efenþeowen	female servant	offestre	foster-mother
firenhicge	harlot/whore/adulteress	plegestre	female athlete
firenhicgend	harlot/whore/adulteress	portcwene	prostitute
fiþelestre	female fiddler	rihtæþelcwen	rightful wife
folccwen	queen/empress	sangestre	female singer
forþwif	wife/married woman; noble lady	scand	harlot/whore/adulteress
fostormodor	foster-mother	scinnlæce	witch/sorceress
freo	female person/woman	scrætte	harlot/whore/adulteress
freodohtor	own daughter	scylcen	loose woman
freowif	free woman	scynnecge	loose woman
frowe	female person/woman	sigewif	witch/sorceress
galdricge	enchantress	steopdohtor	stepdaughter
gefædre	godmother	sunucennicge	mother of a son
geomeowle	old woman	þenestre	female servant
geongre	woman deputy/stewardess	þeodcwen	queen/empress
gesinge	wife/married woman	þinen	female servant
hæmedwif	wife/married woman	þir	female servant
heahrun	enchantress	þyften	female servant
hearpestre	female harpist	timpestre	female player
hellerune	enchantress	unrihtwif	mistress
helrynegu	enchantress	wilnincel	female servant
hleapestre	female dancer	witege	prophetess
hordestre	woman deputy/stewardess	widuwe	widow
hore	harlot/whore/adulteress	wyrtgælstre	witch who works with herbs
hyseberþre	mother of a son	–	–

Table 3 The final dataset taken into account in the study

Word group	Female-gendered terms	Equivalent male-gendered terms
general terms	*wif* 'woman' (1,404), *fæmne* 'woman, girl, maiden' (313) *wifmann* 'woman, female servant' (118)	*wer* 'man' (1,732)
parent	*modor* 'mother' (530)	*fæder* 'father' (2,162)
child	*mægden* 'girl, maiden' (430), *dohtor* 'daughter' (380)	*sunu* 'son' (1,889), *cnapa* 'boy, servant' (152)
sibling	*sweostor* 'sister, nun' (190)	*broþor* 'brother, monk' (1,281)
person with a higher social position	*cwen* 'queen, noblewoman' (172), *hlæfdige* 'lady, noblewoman' (60), *abbodesse* 'abbess' (69), *nunne* 'nun' (52)	*cyning* 'king' (4,599), *hlaford* 'lord' (754), *abbod* 'abbot' (575), *munuc* 'monk' (442)

Table 3 presents the final selection of female-gendered nouns with the male-gendered terms chosen on the basis of their semantic equivalence.[4] The numbers in brackets represent corpus frequencies of the terms. We decided to set the frequency threshold at fifty (which makes *nunne* 'nun' with the frequency of fifty-two the least frequent item in the dataset) since less frequent terms failed to render a substantial number of recurrent collocations in VARIOE.

As shown in Table 3, the terms were grouped into five main categories (some of which are represented by single nouns): general terms, parents, children/young adults, siblings and people of higher social status. The last group is most varied but we wanted to see how social position interacts with gender in the Anglo-Saxon context, and the results (cf. Sections 3.1.5, 3.3.5, 4.1.5 and 4.2.5) show that this particular category is really interesting.

The recently released VARIOE dictionary of OE collocations (Pęzik & Cichosz, 2021), which was the primary tool used for the research presented in this Element, is based on lemmatised YCOE data – that is, every word form in the corpus was aligned to its base form, which for nouns means the singular nominative form with the dominant spelling. This is a prerequisite

---

[4] It is important to note that we have decided not to take the word *man* 'man, human' into account since in OE it had two basic senses and it was very often used as the gender-neutral term for a human being.

of any phraseological study since OE, as an inflected language, uses a great variety of morphological forms for nouns, adjectives, pronouns and verbs. Moreover, without a spelling standard, the lexemes may appear in many different spelling forms, which increases the variation and makes lemmatisation even more important because without it, it would be impossible to perform any kind of automated searches of recurrent collocations.[5] In addition, OE inflections allowed for a relatively flexible sentence structure and a collocation does not necessarily follow a fixed word order – for example, an adjective could both precede and follow a noun, an object could be placed both before and after a lexical verb, etcetera. VARIOE takes this flexibility into consideration, searching for a given part of speech in close proximity to another one, allowing for intervening phrases and changes in relative order.[6] The collocation patterns offered by VARIOE that we have decided to use are:

ADJ + N: an adjective preceding or following a noun (irrespective of case, with some intervening elements possible), for example, *(se) halga gast* '(the) holy ghost'

GEN + N: a genitive noun in close proximity to a head noun (irrespective of case, with intervening elements possible), for example, *Godes gast* 'God's spirit'

N + CONJ + N: two nouns linked by a conjunction (irrespective of case, with some intervening elements possible), for example, *dæg and niht* 'day and night'

---

[5] For example, the phrase *eallmihtig God* 'almighty God' appears in the following morphological and spelling variants in YCOE: *ælmihtiga God, ælmihtigan Godes, ælmihtigne God, ælmeahtegum Gode, ælmihtigan Gode, ælmihtega God, ælmehteges Godes, ælmihtegum Gode, ælmihti God, ealmihtigne Godd, ælmihtig God, aelmaehtgan Godes, almihtigæ God, ælmigtiga God, hælmihtiga God, ælmihtgan Gode, ealmihtiga God, ælmyhtyga God, ælmyhtegan God, almihtig God, ealmihtigne God, ælmihtigon Gode*.

[6] As in the case of *fon to rice* 'take to power' (i.e. 'become a ruler'), illustrated by (i)–(iv), which show four variants from the same text, i.e. Bede's *Historia Ecclesiastica*, extracted by VARIOE.

(i)   æfter   his   fæder   to   rice   feng
     and   after   his   father   to   power   took
     'And (he) took the throne after his father' (cobede,Bede_1:8.42.17.355)

(ii) **feng**   to   rice   Honorius   casere
     took   to   power   Honorius   emperor
     'Honorius became emperor' (cobede,Bede_1:9.42.24.361)

(iii) Eadbald   his   sunu   **feng**   to   ðam   rice
     Eadbald   his   sone   took   to   the   power
     'His sone Eadbald succeeded to the throne' (cobede,Bede_2:5.110.22.1042)

(iv) &   his   sunu   Cænwalh   **feng**   to   his   rice
     and   his   son   Canwalh   took   to   his   power
     'And his son Canwalh succeeded to the throne' (cobede,Bede_3:5.168.15.1633)

V + N: a verb form (finite or non-finite) in close proximity to a noun in the dative, accusative or genitive case (with some intervening elements possible), for example, *lufian God* 'to love God'

N + V: a noun in the nominative case in close proximity to a verb form (finite or non-finite) (with some intervening elements possible), for example, *God cwæð* 'God said'.

Since recurrent patterns returned by VARIOE are based on linear co-occurrence, some of the results are linguistic noise that needs to be filtered out. Thus each collocation had to be inspected in context, and on the basis of the analysis of examples we decided whether a given pair of words may indeed be treated as a collocational pattern.[7] All the data shown in Sections 3 and 4 underwent this clean-up operation and the results can reliably be treated as fully-fledged collocations of the gendered OE nouns analysed in this Element. In the analysis we focus on recurrent patterns – that is, for a collocation to qualify for further processing, it needed to appear at least twice in the YCOE corpus.

The analysis is illustrated with numbered YCOE corpus examples. Following the Leipzig glossing rules, the first line of each example is the original OE text, the second line provides a word-by-word gloss, while the third line is an idiomatic present-day English translation. Every example contains a YCOE identifier, which shows the text file name, for example, cobede for Bede's *Ecclesiastical History*, and the numbers indicating the precise location of the fragment in the OE manuscript.

During the analysis, all of the identified collocations were subjected to a simple semantic analysis in order to identify the main tendencies in the data. In the case of adjectives, the lexemes were divided into positive (indicating an objectively positive trait of a person in the early medieval Christian context, such as *good*, *pious* or *law-abiding*), negative (indicating an objectively negative trace of character, such as *cruel*, *evil* or *dishonest*), physical (related to physicality and general appearance, such as *beautiful*, *old* or *pregnant*) and neutral (including quantifier-like adjectives such as *other*, *same* or *next*, indicating other features such as ethnicity, religious denomination, social position, financial situation, e.g. *Hebrew* or *poor*, as well as any adjective nor fitting the other categories, e.g. *eternal*).

The genitival modifiers were also divided into a few semantic groups based around family (indicating all sorts of family relations, e.g. *someone's wife,*

---

[7] For example, the search for the use of the noun *cyning* 'king' as an object returns the pattern *sprecan + cyning* 'to speak + king', which after a closer inspection is a false hit since *cyning* is here a genitival modifier of another noun. Since some OE verbs take genitive objects, the underlying VARIOE query returns such examples, which need to be eliminated manually.

brother or *child*), faith (centred around God or the Catholic Church, e.g. *God's woman, abbess of the monastery*), body (parts of the body or inner organs, e.g. *someone's eyes, heart* or *blood*) and power (describing someone's authority in the form of *orders, possession, servants* or *office*), with 'other' as the category covering all the remaining semantic fields.

In the case of verb-based collocations, both with subjects and objects, the classification relies on the verb and includes some basic categories such as being (*to be, to become*), saying (*to speak, to answer*), possession (both as a stable state, e.g. *to have, to own*, and the process of transfer, e.g. *to give*), state (both stable, e.g. *to live*, and the process of change, e.g. *to grow, to die*), motion (*to go, to leave, to sit down*), cognition (*to think, to understand*), perception (*to see, to hear*), emotion (*to love, to hate*) or commitment (*to promise, to swear*), as well as verbs in the passive voice and modal verbs.

All the tables provide frequency (total number of attestations in the corpus), though for reasons of clarity, in most tables only the data above a certain frequency threshold are presented, which is clearly indicated in the table captions. However, the analysis takes all the recurrent collocations into account, and all the figures presented in Sections 3 and 4 are based on the complete dataset.

3 Collocations on the Level of the Noun Phrase

3.1 Adjectival Modifiers (A + N and N + A)

3.1.1 General Nouns

The first category of collocations that we extracted from the YCOE corpus are recurrent adjective + noun combinations. In the case of the basic woman terms – that is, *wif, fæmne* and *wifmann* – there are 52 recurrent collocations of this type, amounting to 317 tokens in total (see table 4), which we classified as neutral, positive, negative or physical, according to the methodology presented in Section 2.

It is interesting to note that among the most frequent collocations there is one extremely negative (*yfel* 'evil') and one extremely positive (*halig* 'holy'), as illustrated by (1) and (2).

(1) Eornostlice   nis   nan   wyrmcynn.   ne   wildeora   cyn.
    truly   not-is   no   snake-kind   nor   wild-animal   kind
    on   yfelnysse   gelic   **yfelum**   **wife**
    on   evilness   similar evil   woman
    'Truly, there is no kind of snake or wild animal similar in their evilness to an evil woman.' (cocathom1,+ACHom_I,_32:457.186.6500)

Table 4 Most frequent adjectival collocates of *wif, fæmne* and *wifmann*[8] 'woman' (> 5) in YCOE

Number	Lemma[9]	Translation	Category	Σ
1	halig+fæmne	holy woman	positive	53
2	oþer+wif	other woman	neutral	32
3	eadig+fæmne	blessed woman	positive	24
4	clæne+fæmne	immaculate woman	physical	20
5	earm+wif	poor woman	neutral	13
6	yfel+wif	evil woman	negative	12
7	halig+wif	holy woman	positive	11
8	agen+wif	own woman	neutral	10
9	æþele+fæmne	noble woman	positive	9
10	æwfæst+wif	religious woman	positive	6
11	cristen+wif	Christian woman	neutral	6
12	eald+wif	old woman	physical	6
13	chanaeisc+wif	Canaanite woman	neutral	5
14	samaritanisc+ wif	Samaritan woman	neutral	5
–	other	–	–	105
–	total recurrent	–	–	317

(2) Ðæt   on   Berccingum þam   mynster mid   heofonlice leohte
     that   on   Berching   the   monastery with   heavenly   light
     getacnod wæs, hwær   gesette beon   sceoldon þa   lichaman
     shown   was where   placed be   should   the   bodies
     haligra   fæmnena.
     holy.GEN   women.GEN
     'How heavenly light showed the place where the bodies of holy women should be buried in the Berching monastery.' (cobede,BedeHead:4.18.15.90)

Next, it should be indicated that there is a relatively high proportion of adjectives describing physicality, many of which are related to a woman's ability or inability to bear children: *clæne* 'clean, pure, immaculate', *eald* 'old', *blind*

---

[8] Since *wifmann* is a lower-frequency noun, its collocations are also relatively infrequent and none of them reaches the frequency threshold of five, which means that all of them belong to the category 'other'. The same situation may be observed in Table 9 (with *cnapa* 'boy'), Table 16 (*wifmann* 'woman'), Table 21 (*cnapa* 'boy'), Table 25 (*munuc* 'monk' and *hlaford* 'lord'), Table 26 (*wifmann* 'woman'), Table 31 (*cnapa* 'boy'), Table 34 (*hlæfdige* 'lady'), Table 36 (*wifmann* 'woman') and Table 44 (*abbod* 'abbot' and *munuc* 'monk').

[9] As explained in Section 2, VARIOE returns results in the form of lemmas (normalised basic word forms with singular nominative forms for nouns and their modifiers, infinitives for verbs and the dominant spelling forms for uninflected parts of speech).

'blind',[10] *bearneaca* 'pregnant, big with child', *dead* 'dead', *bearneacnigende* 'pregnant, child-carrying', *unwæstmbære* 'sterile', *untimende* 'barren', *fæger* 'fair, beautiful', as illustrated in (3). It is noteworthy that the concern with female physicality focuses on nothing else but women's reproductive potential.

(3) and   æfter   þam   Boclican   regole,   ne   sceolde   nan   man
     and   after   the   biblical   rule   not   should   no   man
     bearneacnigendum wife   genealæcan,   Ne   monoðseocum, ne   þam
     pregnant   woman   approach   nor   month-sick   nor this
     ðe   for   ylde   untymende   byð.
     that   for   age   barren   is
     'And according to the Bible, no man should have sexual intercourse with a pregnant woman or a menstruating one, or the one who is barren because of old age.' (coaelhom,+AHom_20:111.2991)

Moreover, a few adjectives apart from *yfel* 'evil' are clearly negative – that is, *synfull* 'sinful,' *deofolseoc* 'devil-sick', *ungeleafull* 'unbelieving', see (4) – while the positive ones are related to a woman's obedience to the rules and the regulations of the Christian faith: *halig* 'holy', *arwurþ* 'honourable', *æwfæst* 'pious', *geleafful* 'righteous', *god* 'good', *æw* 'lawful', *æþele* 'noble'. The negative adjectives, then, relate mostly to a woman's deviation from faith and her consequent iniquities, while the positive ones are very broad in meaning and they do not reveal much about the qualities of the woman's character or about her skills, as in (5).

(4) Ac   wite   þu   man   Þæt   ic   eom   **synful**   **wif**
     but   know   you   man   that   I   am   sinful   woman
     'But you should know, man, that I am a sinful woman.' (comary,LS_23_[MaryofEgypt]:284.191)

(5) Þa   wiston   hi,   þæt   þær   neah   wunode   sum   **eawfæst**
     Then   knew   they   that   there near   lived   some   pious
     wif.
     woman
     'Then they learned that a pious woman lived nearby.' (cogregdH,GD_2_[H]:12.126.25.1205)

All in all, the majority of adjectives used to describe *wif* 'woman' are positive or neutral in meaning (39 per cent and 37 per cent respectively), 6 per cent are negative, while as many as 18 per cent are related to the woman's physicality

---

[10] As explained in Section 2, many of the recurrent collocations discussed in Sections 3 and 4 have a frequency below five, so they are usually not included in the tables, but all of them are taken into account in the figures. In this case, *blind* + *wif* 'blind woman' has a frequency of four, so it does not appear in Table 4.

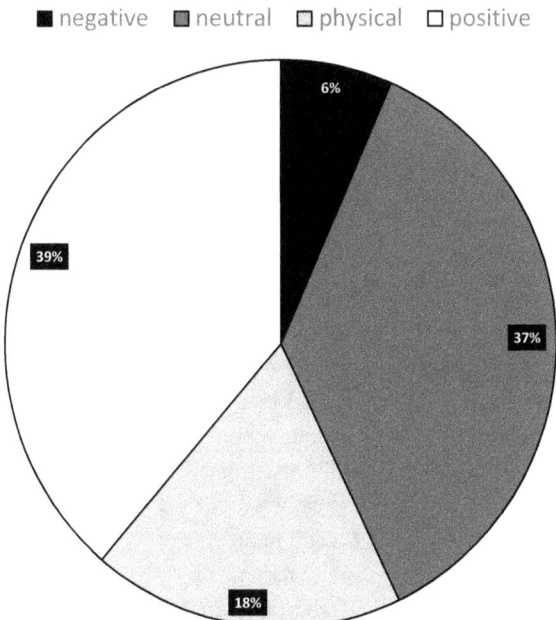

Figure 1 Semantic categories of recurrent adjectival collocates of *wif, fæmne* and *wifmann* 'woman' in YCOE.

(cf. Figure 1). By contrast, the collocations of *wer* 'man' are predominantly positive, as shown in Table 5 and illustrated with (6).

(6) | Mine | gebroðra. | we | rædað | nu | æt | Godes | ðenungum |
|---|---|---|---|---|---|---|---|
| my | brothers | we | read | now | at | God's | service |
| be | ðan | **eadigan** | **were** | IOB. | | | |
| about | the | blessed | man | Job | | | |

'My brothers, during the God's service we will read about the blessed man Job.' (cocathom2,+ACHom_II,_35:260.1.5801)

Apart from the dominance of adjectives with clearly positive connotations, the list notably lacks any lexemes describing a man's physicality. The only two exceptions are *strang* 'strong' and *eald* 'old', both extremely rare considering the generally high frequency of *wer* in the corpus, and neither of them referring to a man's sexuality, unlike the adjectives collocating with the women terms. Moreover, negatively connotating adjectives are also practically absent from the study sample, with *blodig* 'cruel' and *unrihtwis* 'unrighteous' representing this rare pattern. Interestingly, two out of these four infrequent collocations – that is, *strang* 'strong' and *blodig* 'cruel' – have connotations befitting the stipulated warrior's position and signalling power and hardness, cf. (7) and (8). Such instances are not attested with women terms.

Table 5 Most frequent adjectival collocates of *wer* 'man' (> 5) in YCOE

Number	Lemma	Translation	Category	Σ
1	*halig+wer*	holy man	positive	453
2	*arwurþ+wer*	honourable man	positive	144
3	*eadig+wer*	blessed man	positive	54
4	*ilca+wer*	same man	neutral	39
5	*æþele+wer*	noble man	positive	28
6	*god+wer*	good man	positive	26
7	*æwfæst+wer*	pious man	positive	21
8	*oþer+wer*	other man	neutral	17
9	*mære+wer*	great man	positive	15
10	*æfæst+wer*	pious man	positive	11
11	*geleafful+wer*	faithful man	positive	10
12	*hæþen+wer*	heathen man	neutral	8
13	*swilc+wer*	such man	neutral	7
14	*rihtwis+wer*	righteous man	positive	7
15	*agen+wer*	(sb's) own man	neutral	5
16	*beorht+wer*	glorious man	positive	5
17	*apostolic+wer*	apostolic man	neutral	5
18	*geþyldig+wer*	patient man	positive	5
–	other	–	–	60
–	all recurrent	–	–	920

(7) Ða   synd   **blodige** **weras** ðe   wyrcað manslihtas,   and   ða
    these   are   cruel   men   who   do   man-slaughters   and   these
    ðe   manna   sawla   beswicað   to   forwyrde.
    that men's   souls   lead   to   destruction
    'These are cruel men who commit murder and these who lead people's souls to destruction.'(coaelive,+ALS[Pr_Moses]:305.3038)

(8) Þæt   wæron   **strange**   **weras**   ond   sigefæste   on   woroldgefeohtum
    that   were   strong   men   and   victorious   in   world-fights
    'These were strong men, victorious in worldly fights.' (comart3,Mart_5_[Kotzor]:Ma9,A.3.326)

All in all, as shown in Figure 2, the adjectival collocates of *wer* are predominantly positive, and the difference between the analysed terms is really striking. As can been seen, then, the comparison of adjectival collocates of general OE terms describing women and men shows a significant difference in the linguistic image of both sexes. Men are mostly described in

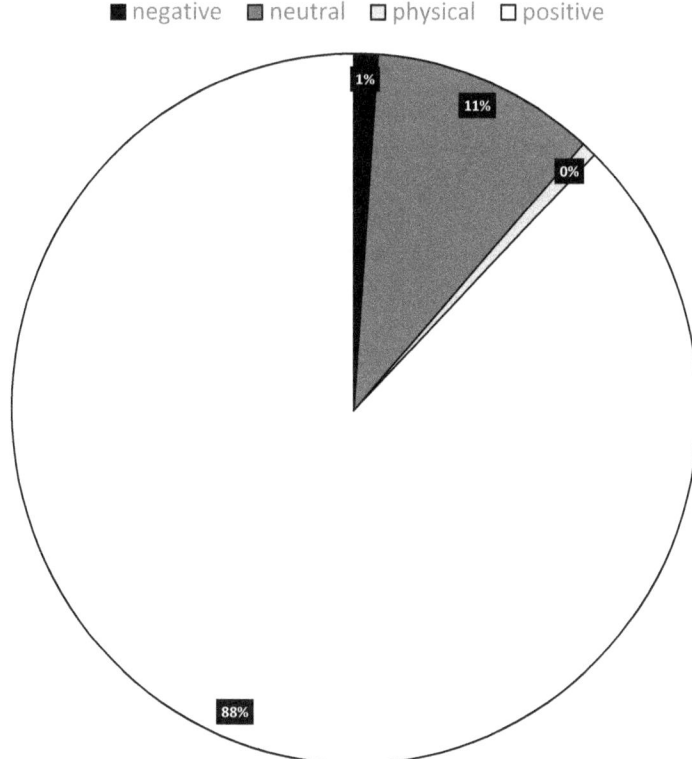

Figure 2 Semantic categories of recurrent adjectival collocates of *wer* 'man' in YCOE.

unreservedly positive terms, and even if not, the focus remains on their warrior qualities. Women, in contrast, are frequently valued in (morally) negative terms. An interesting group of collocates consists of adjectives related to the body, which in the Christian tradition is perceived as an imperfect part of a human being and a source of corruption; the particular sphere of interest is the reproductive capability, which signals the instrumental quality of the woman.

3.1.2 Parent Terms

The next gendered noun pair in the analysis is *modor* 'mother' and *fæder* 'father'. Table 6 reveals that in the case of the former, adjectival collocations are not very numerous. What is more, many instances of *modor* are in fact references to Mary, the mother of Christ, which includes all the occurrences of *halig* 'holy' and *eadig* 'blessed', as in (9).

Table 6 Recurrent adjectival collocates of *modor* 'mother' in YCOE

Number	Adjective	Translation	Category	Σ
1	*halig+modor*	holy mother	positive	11
2	*gastlic+modor*	spiritual mother	neutral	10
3	*agen+modor*	own mother	neutral	10
4	*eald+modor*	old mother	physical	5
5	*ilca+modor*	same mother	neutral	4
6	*eadig+modor*	blessed mother	positive	3
7	*leof+modor*	beloved mother	positive	3
8	*cristen+modor*	Christian mother	neutral	3
9	*lichamlic+modor*	physical mother	neutral	2
10	*dreorig+modor*	sorrowful mother	neutral	2
11	*eorþlic+modor*	earthly mother	neutral	2
12	*ærest+modor*	first mother	neutral	2
–	total recurrent	–	–	57

(9) Seo **halige moder** Maria þa afedde þæt cyld mid micelre
the holy mother Mary then fed the child with great
arwyrðnysse.
reverence
'The holy mother Mary then fed the child with great reverence.' (cocathom1, +ACHom_I,_1:187.246.258)

What is more, the spiritual mother (*gastlice modor*), which is the second most frequent adjectival collocation in Table 6, is actually a metaphor denoting the Catholic Church (cf. (10)).

(10) Ealle we habbað ænne **heofonlicne fæder** and ane **gastlice**
oh we have one heavenly father and one spiritual
modor, seo is ecclesia genamod, þæt is
mother that is ecclesia called that is
Godes cirice, and þa we sculon æfre lufian and wurðian.
God's church and these we should always love and honour
'Indeed we have a heavenly father and a spiritual mother called *ecclesia*, which means God's church, and we should always love and honour them.' (coinspolD, WPol_2.1.2_[Jost]:99.140)

The most frequent reference to physicality is the adjective *eald* 'old', though in two cases the referent is Eve, the mother of all people, as in (11).

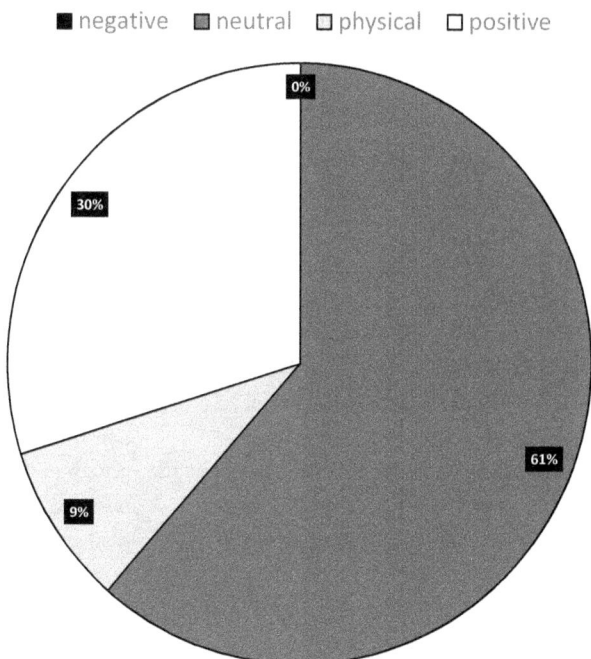

Figure 3 Semantic categories of recurrent adjectival collocates of *modor* 'mother' in YCOE.

(11) Ure **ealde moder** Eua us beleac heofenan rices
our old mother Eve us locked heaven kingdom
geat.
gate
'Our old (original) mother Eve locked the door to the kingdom of heaven for us.'
(cocathom2,+ACHom_II,_1:11.295.244)

Figure 3 shows that the distribution of collocation types for *modor* is drastically different from the one obserwed in *wer* (Figure 2) since the proportion of positive collocations is almost three times lower (30 per cent vs. 88 per cent). Compared to the general women terms shown in Figure 1, there is a visibly lower proportion of physical collocations, which is clearly the result of the strong presence of St. Mary in this category. Naturally, the linguistic image of the mother of Christ does not concentrate on her body. (However, as later analysis will show, the corpus contains references to her womb.)

As far as *fæder* 'father' is concerned, the most striking observation is the high frequency of the analysed pattern compared to *modor* (457 vs. 57 recurrent collocations).

Table 7 Most frequent adjectival collocates of *fæder* 'father' (> 5) in YCOE

Number	Lemma	Translation	Category	Σ
1	heofonlic+fæder	heavenly father	neutral	87
2	halig+fæder	holy father	positive	84
3	eallmihtig+fæder	almighty father	positive	69
4	arwurþ+fæder	noble father	positive	51
5	ilca+fæder	same father	neutral	25
6	eald+fæder	old father	physical	22
7	leof+fæder	dear father	positive	21
8	god+fæder	good father	positive	14
9	agen+fæder	own father	neutral	10
10	ece+fæder	eternal father	neutral	8
11	wis+fæder	wise father	positive	8
12	mildheort+fæder	merciful father	positive	6
13	arfæst+fæder	honourable father	positive	5
14	soþ+fæder	true father	positive	5
–	other	–	–	42
–	total recurrent	–	–	457

Table 7 shows quite clearly that many of these are references to God, the father of all people, described as holy, almighty and eternal (cf. (12))

(12) Crist   is   ancenned   Sunu of þam **ælmihtigan Fæder**;
     Christ is   only begotten   son   of the   almighty   father
     'Christ is the only begotten son of the almighty Father.' (coaelhom, +AHom_1:386.199)

Interestingly, the phrase *leof fæder* ('dear father') is often a vocative phrase directed at God, as in (13).

(13) **leof   fæder**, we geanbidodon, þæt þu   come, swa swa þu
     dear   father   we waited   that you   come   so   as   you
     behete ...
     promised
     'Dear Father, we waited for you to come as you promised ... ' (cogregdH, GD_2_[H]:22.148.24.1463)

In (14) *eald* 'old' refers to (numerous) male ancestors: this marks a difference to the collocation *eald modor* 'old mother', which usually refers to Eve, as in (11). Apparently, collectively understood familial ancestry is conceptualised only in paternal terms.

Representations of Women in Old English Prose 27

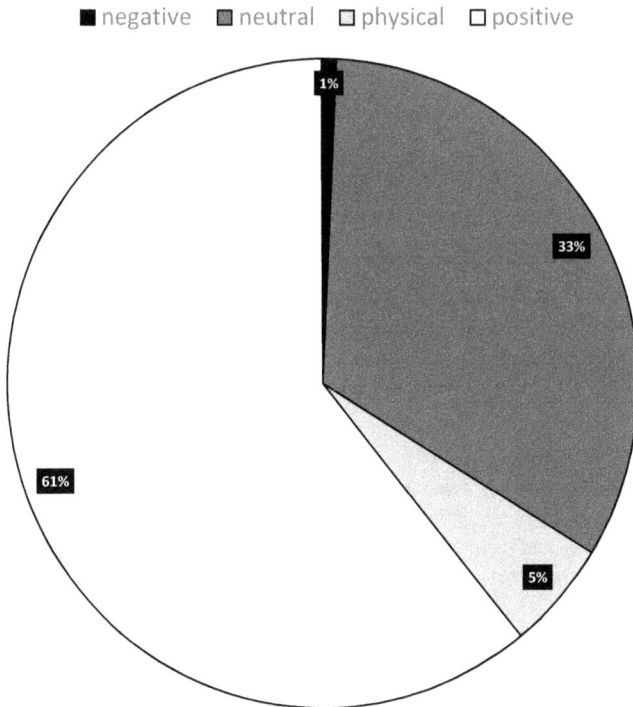

Figure 4 Semantic categories of recurrent adjectival collocates of *fæder* 'father' in YCOE.

(14) Hwæt hit is gesæd ðæt ure **ealdan fæderas** wæron
 what it is said that our old fathers were
 ceapes hierdas.
 cattle keepers
 'What! It is said that our old fathers (ancestors) were cowherds.' (cocura, CP:17.109.4.716)

Figure 4 shows that, again, the proportion of positive adjectives is much higher for the male term (61 per cent for *fæder* and only 30 per cent for *modor*), and adjectives related to physicality are marginally used in the case of men (only 5 per cent).

The collocation analysis of the two parental terms yields results similar to the examination of general female and male terms. It has to be noted, nonetheless, that these findings are of more limited relevance: because of their use in religious contexts, both *modor* and *fæder* have referents which do not relate to the linguistic image of women and men in Old English. An interesting observation concerns the historical lineage of Anglo-Saxon society: given that ancestors are denoted as 'old fathers' and not 'old mothers', it can be assumed that the socio-cultural legacy of Anglo-Saxons was found in paternality, which certainly agrees with a tendency generally observed in other cultures and languages.

3.1.3 Terms Denoting Children and Young Adults

In the 'child and young adult' category illustrated in Table 8, the two female nouns, *mægden* 'maiden' and *dohtor* 'daughter', are regularly presented in the context of their sexual purity (*clæne* 'clean, immaculate' and *ungewemmed* 'untouched, immaculate'). The holy and immaculate maiden is of course the Virgin Mary who became Christ's mother, so once again the data are dominated by a single female referent.

(15) Se   ylca   Godes   sunu   geceas   him   to   meder   þæt   **halige**
     the   same   God's   son   chose   him   to   mother   the   holy
     mæden,   Marian   gehaten
     maiden   Mary   called
     'God's son also chose the holy maiden called Mary to be his mother.' (colwstan1, +ALet_2_[Wulfstan_1]:13.29)

(16) ac   Crist   næs   na   geteald   to   þissere
     but   Christ   not-was   not   included   to   this
     wiðmetenysse,   se   þe   acenned   wæs   of   ðam
     comparison   this   that   born   was   of   the
     clænan   **mædene**.
     clean   maiden
     'But Christ was not included in this comparison, he who was born of the clean maiden.' (colsigewZ,+ALet_4_[SigeweardZ]:855.343)

Table 8 Most frequent adjectival collocates of *mægden* 'maiden' and *dohtor* 'daughter' (> 5) in YCOE

Number	Lemma	Translation	Category	Σ
1	*halig+mægden*	holy maiden	positive	32
2	*clæne+mægden*	immaculate maiden	physical	28
3	*æþele+mægden*	noble maiden	positive	8
4	*leof+dohtor*	dear daughter	positive	8
5	*oþer+mægden*	other maiden	neutral	7
6	*stunt+mægden*	foolish maiden	negative	6
7	*ungewemmed+mægden*	immaculate maiden	physical	5
8	*snotor+mægden*	wise maiden	positive	5
9	*agen+dohtor*	own daughter	neutral	5
–	other	–	–	53
–	total recurrent	–	–	152

Sometimes, though, it is a young female, as in the biblical story about wise and foolish virgins, or in the case of Apollonius of Tyre, where the king's daughter is one of the characters in the story, and *leof* 'dear' is again used in a vocative phrase.

(17) Þa **stuntan** **mædenu** cwædon to ðam **snoterum**;
the stupid maidens said to the wise
'The foolish maidens said to the wise ones' (cocathom2,+ACHom_II, _44:327.14.7348)

(18) and cwæð: **leofe dohtor**, þu gesingodest;
and said dear daughter you sinned
'And said: Dear daughter, you have sinned' (coapollo,ApT:16.2.303)

All in all, positive adjectives are the dominant category (cf. Figure 5). This stems mostly from the fact that the texts in the corpus often accentuate the virginity of maidens and daughters, a characteristic strongly valued by the Christian religion and consequently associated with positive features of character. Again, as with previously examined female nouns, the proportion of adjectives describing physicality is high, amounting here to 31 per cent.

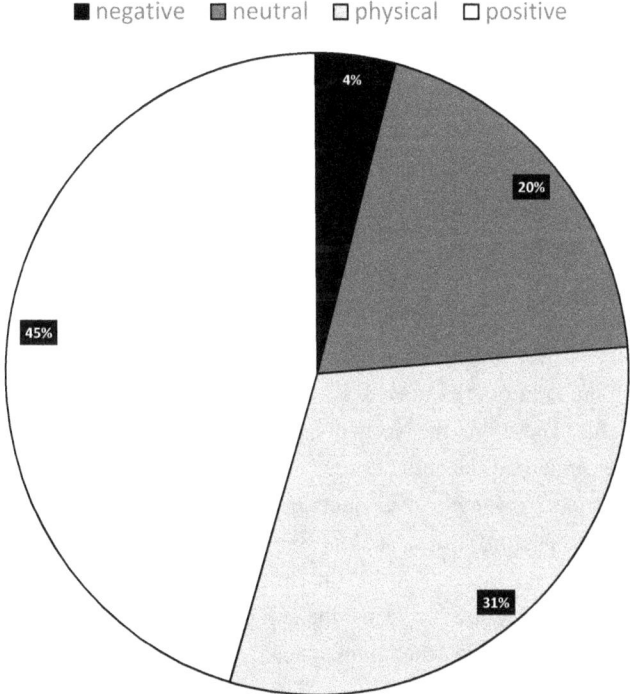

Figure 5 Semantic categories of recurrent adjectival collocates of *mægden* 'maiden' and *dohtor* 'daughter' in YCOE.

Table 9 Most frequent adjectival collocates of *sunu* 'son' and *cnapa* 'boy' (> 5) in YCOE[11]

Number	Lemma	Translation	Category	Σ
1	*ancenned+sunu*	only begotten son	neutral	46
2	*agen+sunu*	own son	neutral	31
3	*oþer+sunu*	other/second son	neutral	23
4	*leof+sunu*	dear son	positive	23
5	*eald+sunu*	old son	physical	13
6	*frumcenned+sunu*	firstborn son	neutral	11
7	*ilca+sunu*	same son	neutral	9
8	*dead+sunu*	dead son	physical	8
9	*geong+sunu*	young son	physical	7
10	*soþ+sunu*	true son	positive	5
–	other	–	–	36
–	total recurrent	–	–	212

In the case of young males, the most frequent adjectives used to describe them can be classified as neutral (cf. Table 9). It is interesting to note, however, that a significant number of them describe the relation of a son to other (usually male) children (*ancenned* 'only begotten', *frumcenned* 'firstborn', *oþer* 'other, second', etc.). This emphasis on the distinction between firstborn and other sons might be linked with the development of a socio-cultural process which will later, in Norman times, lead to introducing primogeniture as a basis of land inheritance. Primogeniture, whose roots might be traced in the Bible, was not universally observed in early medieval Europe: the inheritance laws followed the pattern of Roman law, which did not distinguish between older and younger or between male and female heirs. Yet, the development of the medieval feudal system stipulated that the socio-political power of a lord depended on keeping the land estate large, so its division between family members was not favourable. Therefore, the Norman laws provided that the lord's oldest son, not daughter, inherited the entire estate.

The importance of male over female offspring is visible in the higher frequency of the word *sunu* 'son' (1,889) compared to *dohtor* 'daughter' (380). This does not necessarily result from religious referents: while many uses of *sunu* are references to Jesus, the son of God, most of the collocations listed in Table 9 pertain to other, human sons.

---

[11] As a lower-frequency item, *cnapa* 'boy' fails to show any recurrent collocations with a frequency above five so all the patterns built around this noun are counted in the 'other' category in the table, but its collocates are included in Figure 6.

(19) Æfter   þæm   Lisimachus ofslog his   **agenne** **sunu** Agothoclen &
     after   that   Lisimachus killed his   own   son   Agothoclen and
     Antipater his   aþum.
     Antipater his   son-in-law
     'Afterwards Lisimachus killed his own son Agothoclen and his son-in-law
     Antipater.' (coorosiu,Or_3:11.82.13.1645)

Naturally, Jesus Christ is attested in the data, for example, in (20), but this referent does not dominate in the same way as Mary, the virgin and the mother, dominates the collocation sets for *modor* 'mother' and *mæden* 'maiden'.

(20) &   cwæþ,   her   ys   min   **leofa** **sunu** on   þam   me
     and   said   here   is   my   dear   son   on   whom   me
     wel   gelicaþ;
     well pleases
     'And said: Here is my dear son, in whom I am well pleased.' (cowsgosp,Mt_[WSCp]:17.5.1128)

All the recurrent adjectival collocations combined prove to be mostly neutral in meaning (cf. Figure 6). For male terms, 16 per cent is quite

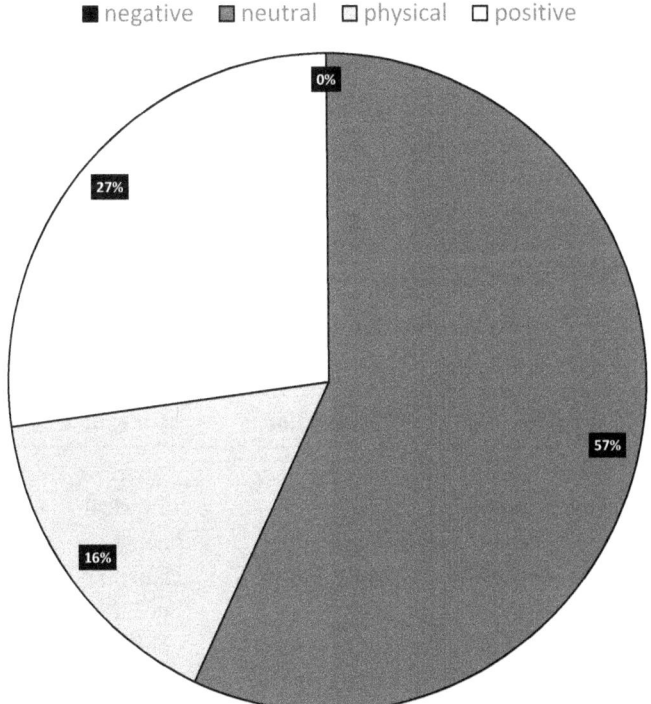

Figure 6 Semantic categories of recurrent adjectival collocates of *sunu* 'son' and *cnapa* 'boy' in YCOE.

a high result for collocates related to physicality, but almost all of them are related to the sons' age or their death; not a single one describes their appearance. Frequently, neutral and physical collocates associate with family seniority, which can have a connection with primogeniture, as indicated previously.

3.1.4 Sibling Terms

The next set of terms from the semantic field 'sibling' prove extremely unevenly represented. In the case of *sweostor* 'sister' there are only three recurrent adjectival collocations amounting to only twelve occurrences in total, all of them completely neutral in meaning, as illustrated by Table 10. The complete asymmetry between *sweostor* and *broþor* is quite clearly indicated by Table 11, with 166 tokens representing the latter.

It is worth noting that most of the brothers referred to in the collocations are monks, disciples and generally 'spiritual brothers' as in (21), more often than actual siblings as in (22), which quite clearly shows the stronger association of females with family life and males with public service.

Table 10 Recurrent adjectival collocates of *sweostor* 'sister' in YCOE

Number	Lemma	Translation	Category	Σ
1	agen+sweostor	own sister	neutral	7
2	ilca+sweostor	same sister	neutral	3
3	oþer+sweostor	other sister	neutral	2
–	total recurrent	–	–	12

Table 11 Most frequent adjectival collocates of *broþor* 'brother' (> 5) in YCOE

Number	Lemma	Translation	Category	Σ
1	oþer+broþor	other brother	neutral	62
2	geong+broþor	young brother	physical	18
3	agen+broþor	own brother	neutral	16
4	ilca+broþor	same brother	neutral	14
5	leof+broþor	dear brother	positive	14
6	eald+broþor	old brother	physical	12
7	dead+broþor	dead brother	physical	10
–	other	–	–	20
–	total recurrent	–	–	166

(21) Þa   cwæþ   Iohannes,   Bletsiað,   **Broþor**   þa   **leofestan**,
    then   said   John   bless   brothers   the   dearest
    urne   God
    our   God

'Then John said: Dear brothers, bless our God.' (coblick,LS_20_[AssumptMor [BlHom_13])

(22) Ic   and   Ionathas,   min   **gingra**   **broðor**,   Farað   to
    I   and   Jonathan   my   younger   brother   go   to
    Galaað   to   afligenne   þa   hæðenan.
    Galatia to   drive away the   heathens.

'I and Jonathan, my younger brother, (will) go to Galatia to drive away the heathens.' (coaelive,+ALS_[Maccabees]:401.5101)

Since many of the OE texts discuss death of monks and their age, the proportion of physical collocates shown in Figure 7 is quite high, but the only lexemes attested in this group are *geong* 'young', *eald* 'old' and *dead* 'dead'.

Generally, it has to be noted that the analysis of the female and male terms in the sibling category does not yield any noteworthy results, mostly due to an insufficient amount of data.

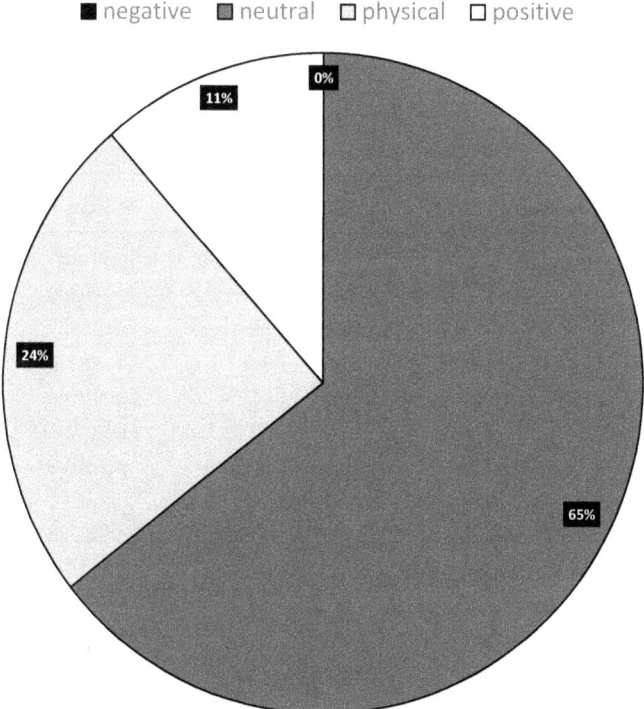

Figure 7 Semantic categories of recurrent adjectival collocates of *broþor* 'brother' in YCOE.

3.1.5 Terms Denoting Women and Men of High Social Status

The last group of gendered nouns represents a different cultural perspective, since it shows a combination of two sociolinguistic features: gender and social position. The category embraces female and male nouns designating people of high social status. The analysis clearly shows that queens, ladies, nuns and abbesses, who were definitely the highest-ranking females in Anglo-Saxon society, do not pattern with other women terms. Table 12 shows that the collocations, infrequent as they are, in most cases are positive and not a single one of them refers to the woman's physicality. It is important to note that the queen or lady referred to in the data is often Mary, the mother of Jesus, as in (23), but the proportions are quite balanced and (24) is a representative example.

(23) ala   þu   **wuldorfæste**   **hlæfdige** þe   þone   soðan   God
     oh   you   glorious   lady   who   the   true   God
     æfter flæsces   gebyrde   acendest...
     after flesh.GEN   origin   bore
     'Oh, you glorious lady, who gave birth to the true God in flesh.' (comary,LS_23_[MaryofEgypt]:431.281)

Table 12 Recurrent adjectival collocates of *cwen* 'queen', *abbodesse* 'abbess', *hlæfdige* 'lady' and *nunne* 'nun' in YCOE

Number	Lemma	Translation	Category	Σ
1	heofonlic+cwen	heavenly queen	neutral	6
2	eadig+cwen	blessed queen	positive	5
3	ilca+cwen	same queen	neutral	4
4	halig+cwen	holy queen	positive	4
5	halig+nunne	holy nun	positive	3
6	ilca+abbodesse	same abbess	neutral	2
7	halig+abbodesse	holy abbess	positive	2
8	arwurþ+abbodesse	honourable abbess	positive	2
9	æþele+abbodesse	noble abbess	positive	2
10	æþele+cwen	noble queen	positive	2
11	god+cwen	good queen	positive	2
12	gastlic+cwen	spiritual queen	neutral	2
13	wuldorfæst+hlæfdige	glorious lady	positive	2
–	total recurrent	–	–	38

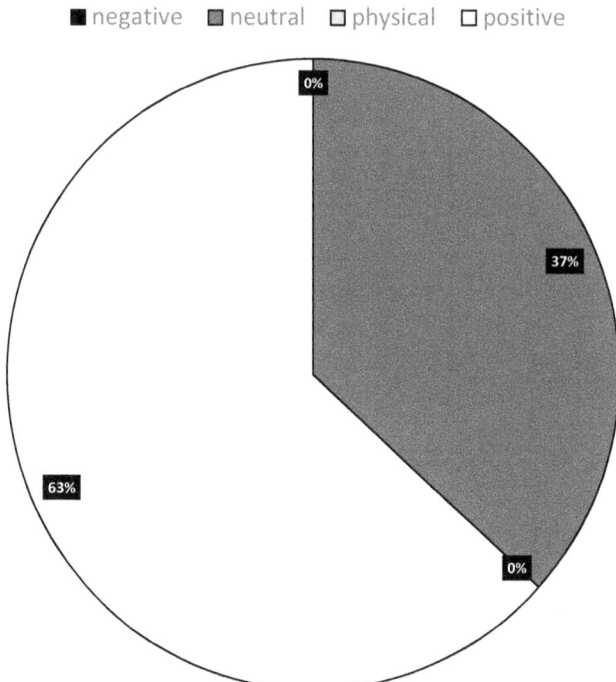

Figure 8 Semantic categories of recurrent adjectival collocates of *cwen* 'queen', *abbodesse* 'abbess', *hlæfdige* 'lady' and *nunne* 'nun' in YCOE.

(24) He   wæs   se   forma   casere   þe   on   Crist   gelyfde,
     he   was   the   first   emperor who   on   Christ believed
     Sancte Elenan sunu, þære   **eadigan cwene**
     Saint Elena son   the   blessed queen
     'He was the first emperor who believed in Christ, the son of Saint Elena, the blessed queen.' (colwstan1,+ALet_2_[Wulfstan_1]:47.87)

When we look at proportions, shown in Figure 8, the graph resembles a typical one for male-gendered nouns, with positive adjectives completely dominating and physical ones absent from the dataset.

In the case of high-ranking males, there is a real abundance of data, with 630 tokens attested and the most frequent ones listed in Table 13. While the heavenly king in (25) is a clear reference to Jesus Christ, and many instances of the lexeme *hlaford* 'lord' as in (26) are references to God, real kings are definitely present in the data (cf. (27) and (28)), and some of them are not positive characters.

Table 13 Most frequent adjectival collocates of *cyning* 'king', *hlaford* 'lord', *abbod* 'abbot' and *munuc* 'monk' (> 10) in YCOE

Number	Lemma	Translation	Category	Σ
1	oþer+cyning	other king	neutral	37
2	heofonlic+cyning	heavenly king	neutral	33
3	ilca+cyning	same king	neutral	26
4	hæþen+cyning	pagan king	neutral	19
5	mære+cyning	great king	positive	17
6	reþe+cyning	just king	positive	16
7	eorþlic+cyning	earthly king	neutral	16
8	cristen+cyning	Christian king	neutral	16
9	soþ+cyning	true king	positive	15
10	god+cyning	good king	positive	15
11	arleas+cyning	honourless king	negative	13
12	leof+hlaford	dear lord	positive	13
13	æþele+cyning	noble king	positive	11
14	oþer+munuc	other monk	neutral	11
15	unrihtwis+cyning	unjust king	negative	10
16	iudeisc+cyning	Jewish king	neutral	10
17	geong+cyning	young king	physical	10
18	halig+abbod	holy abbot	positive	10
–	other	–	–	332
–	total recurrent	–	–	630

(25) & he, se **heofonlica cyning**, þæt eall swiðe
and he the heavenly king, that all very
geðyldelice abær for mancynnes lufan & hælo.
patiently bore for mankind's love and salvation
'And he, the heavenly king, who suffered everything with great patience for the love and salvation of mankind.' (coverhomE,HomS_24.1_[Scragg]:259.232)

(26) We biddað þe, **leof hlaford**, þæt ðu gehyran
we bid you, dear lord, that you hear
wylle ure word.
will our words
'We bid you, dear Lord, that you hear our words.' (cosevensl,LS_34_[SevenSleepers]:273.210)

(27) and þæt word sprang Geond eal þæt land þæt
and the word sprang throughout all the land that
Apollonius, se **mæra cyngc**, Hæfde funden his wif,
Apollonius, the great king had found his wife
'And it became known throughout the land that the great king Apollonius had found a wife.' (coapollo,ApT:49.9.521)

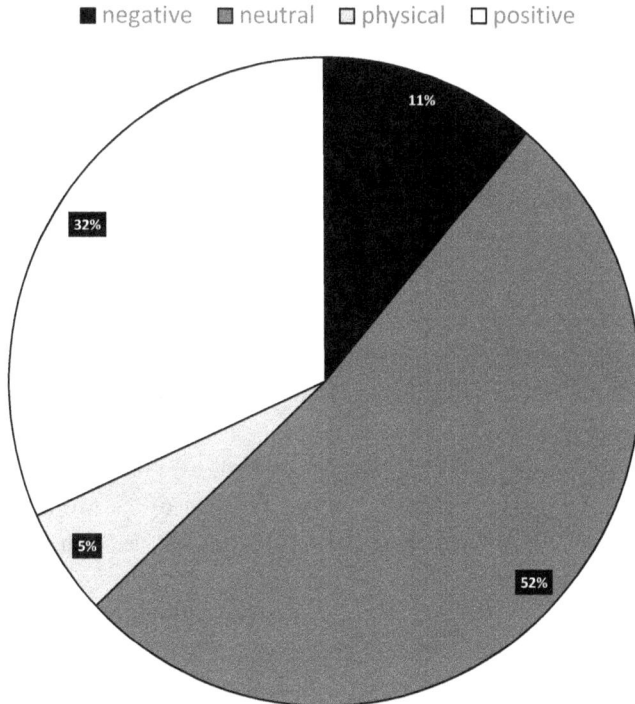

Figure 9 Semantic categories of recurrent adjectival collocates of *cyning* 'king', *hlaford* 'lord', *abbod* 'abbot' and *munuc* 'monk' in YCOE.

(28) Ac on þære nihte þe se **arleasa** **cyning** hine on
but on the night that the honourless king him on
merigen acwellan wolde com Godes engel
morning kill wanted came God's angel
scinende of heofenum
shining of heaven
'But the night before the morning when the honourless king wanted to kill him, God's angel came shining from heaven.' (cocathom1,+ACHom_I, _37:505.240.7503)

Figure 9 shows that while the most frequent adjective category is neutral collocations, the proportion of positive ones is relatively high and, unsurprisingly, modifiers describing physicality are the least numerous group.

The analysis of this category yields particularly interesting results if we examine them against the data from the previous noun groups. It might at first seem paradoxical that high-ranking women have no negative collocates, nor those related to the body. However, since all the referents of female terms examined here are women of an esteemed social status, the results cannot be used to make assumptions about the general position and regard of women in

Anglo-Saxon society. A queen or a lady is not supposed to be described in negative terms, either because she is the mother of Christ or because she is a higher-ranking person than the author of the text. An abbess or a nun, in turn, is part of the religious community of the church, which also guarantees her positive social recognition. Furthermore, the fact that Anglo-Saxon society was stratified means that only average (i.e. low-ranking) women were perceived in terms of their physical qualities.

3.2 Binominals (N + CONJ + N)

Studies show that when two nouns are joined by a conjunction, their order is not random and the factors which play a role in the variation are power or importance (the supreme item comes first), length (the shorter item comes first) and frequency (the more frequent item comes first) (Goldberg & Lee, 2021). Therefore, for instance, when we compare the order of the two most general gendered nouns, *wif* and *wer*, bearing in mind that they are both one-syllable, three-sound words and that the frequency of their designates is comparable, a visible preference of one over the other in the initial position may only be interpreted as difference in power and importance. Table 14 shows very clearly that in the patterns involving two grown-up people of different gender, the male term virtually always comes first, as in (29) and (30).

(29) Wæron his **fæder** & his **modor** buta hæðen.
 were his father and his mother both heathen
 'His father and his mother were both heathen.' (coverhom,LS_17.2_[MartinVerc_18]:9.2230)

(30) And hi ðær genamon inne ealle þa gehadodan
 and they there took in all the ordained
 men and **weras** **and** **wif**
 people and men and women
 'And they took in all the ordained people, both men and women.' (cochronC, ChronC_[Rositzke]:1011.21.1522)

Figure 10 proves that the difference is quite overwhelming. When a pair consists of a female and a male, the order prioritising the male is ten times more frequent (58 per cent vs. 6 per cent). The discrepancy becomes much more striking when we consider that the order privileging women occurs only in the pairs *modor+and+gebroþor* and *modor+and+broþor* – that is, mother and brother – in which the female is favoured not because of the gender but due to her age and family position. This is analogous to *wif+and+cild*, where a woman is phrase-initial when occurring with the gender-neutral child. However, when a child is male, both orders are attested (cf. (31) and (32)).

Table 14 The most frequent binominals with women terms (> 5) in YCOE

Number	Lemma	Translation	Order	Σ
1	fæder+and+modor	father and mother	male > female	68
2	wif+and+cild	woman and child	female > child	35
3	sunu+and+dohtor	son and daughter	male > female	21
4	wer+and+wif	man and woman	male > female	21
5	fæder+oþþe+modor	father or mother	male > female	16
6	modor+and+gebroþor	mother and brother	female > male	13
7	ge+wer+ge+wif[12]	man and woman	male > female	11
8	broþor+and+sweostor	brother and sister	male > female	7
9	ealdormann+and+sweostor	nobleman and sister	male > female	7
10	modor+and+broþor	mother and brother	female > male	6
11	sunu+oþþe+dohtor	son or daughter	male > female	6
12	wif+and+dohtor	woman and daughter	female > child	6
13	cild+and+modor	child and mother	child > female	5
14	ge+wæpenmann+ge+wifmann	men and women	male > female	5
15	wif+and+bearn	woman and son	female > child	5
16	wif+oþþe+bearn	woman or son	female > child	5
–	other	–	–	104
–	all recurrent	–	–	341

(31)   &   ðu   gæst   in   to   ðam   arce,   &   ðine   **suna,**
       and   you   go   in   to   the   ark   and   your   sons
       &   ðin   **wif**   &   ðinra   suna   wif   mid   ðe.
       and   your   woman   and   your   sons'   women   with   you
'And you shall go into the ark, and your sons and your wife and your sons' wives with you.' (cootest,Gen:6.18.294)

(32)   &   Hæstenes   **wif**   &   his   **suna**   twegen   mon   brohte
       And   Hasten's   woman   and   his   sons   two   one   brought
       to   þæm   cyninge
       to   the   king
'And Hasten's wife and his two sons were brought to the king.' (cochronA-2a, ChronA_[Plummer]:894.52.1057)

In the case of male-gendered nouns (Table 15 and Figure 11), it is not only the male > female order which is visible in the data. Another phenomenon which

---

[12] The correlative conjunction 'ge ... ge ... ' works in a way similar to the Modern English 'both ... and ... '

Table 15 The most frequent binominals with men terms (> 10) in YCOE

Number	Lemma	Pattern	Order	Σ
1	fæder+and+modor	father and mother	male > female	68
2	fæder+and+sunu	father and son	two males	63
3	wer+and+wif	man and woman	male > female	21
4	sunu+and+dohtor	son and daughter	male > female	21
5	cyning+and+wita	king and wise man	two males	18
6	sunu+and+gast	son and (holy) ghost	male > other	17
7	fæder+oþþe+modor	father or mother	male > female	16
8	cyning+and+ealdormann	king and nobleman	two males	16
9	cyning+and+eorl	king and earl	two males	15
10	ge+wer+ge+wif	man and woman	male > female	11
11	god+and+fæder	God and father	God > male	10
–	other	–	–	192
–	total recurrent	–	–	468

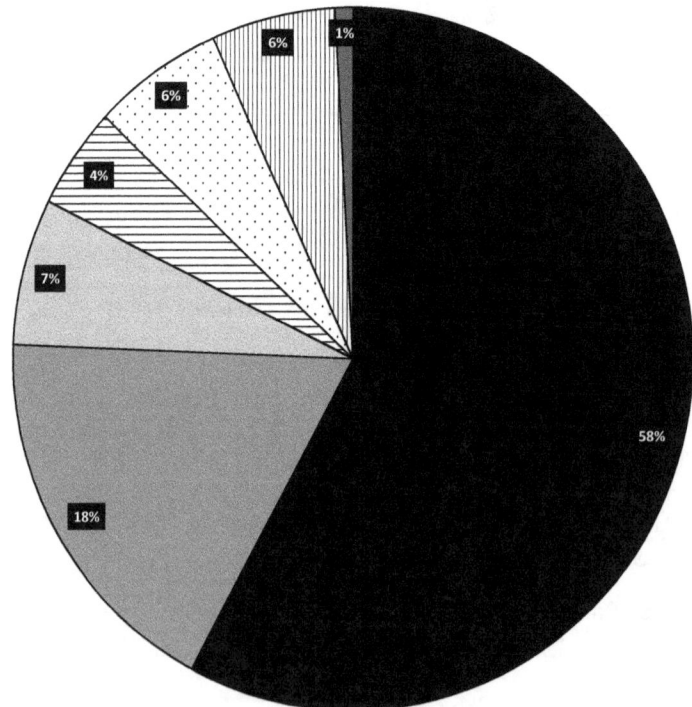

Figure 10 Recurrent binominals with female nouns in YCOE.

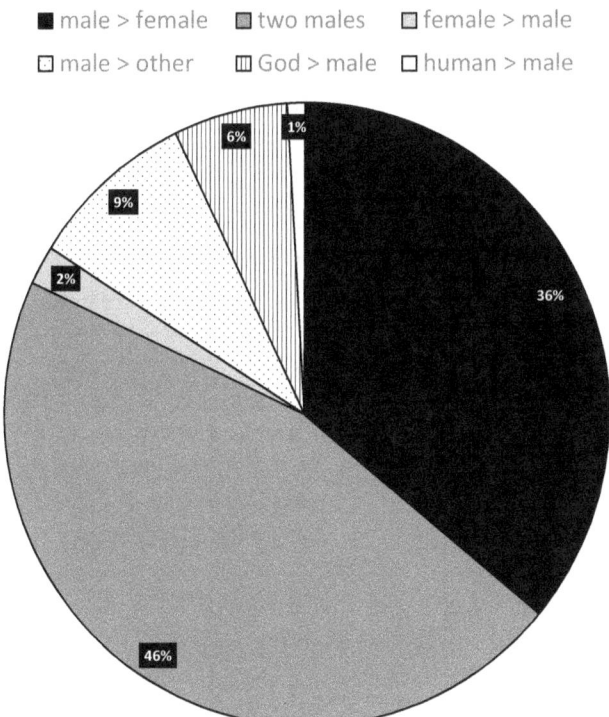

Figure 11 Recurrent binominals with male nouns in YCOE.

surfaces is the frequent pairing of two male terms (e.g. *fæder and sunu* 'father and son'). Importantly, at the same time, such binominals are infrequent in the case of women terms: while there are as many as 213 male + male binominals in the YCOE corpus, the equivalent figure for women is only 16. This could suggest that the units consisting of two people are in most cases culturally relevant only as long as at least one of the persons in the pair is male. Finally, it is interesting to note the absence of any binominals involving a grown-up man and a child, which is in sharp contrast to the high co-ocurrence of women with children and explicitly testifies to a strong socio-cultural connection of women with household and family and, likewise, to men's separation from this sphere of life experience.

3.3 Genitives (GEN + N)

3.3.1 General Terms

In the case of genitival modification, a gendered noun may be both the head noun (e.g., woman in *mannes wif* 'man's woman') and the modifier (e.g., woman in *wifes meolc* 'woman's milk'). Table 16 shows that for the neutral female terms which are heads of the investigated phrases the modifiers are all human (or divine)

Table 16 Genitival modification of and with *wif, fæmne* and *wifmann* 'woman' (> 5) in YCOE

Number	Lemma	Translation	Group	Σ
1	*Godes fæmne*	God's woman	faith	34
2	*mannes wif*	man's woman	family	12
3	*fæmnan mynster*	woman's monastery	faith	10
4	*wifes meolc*	woman's milk	body	9
5	*wifes bearn*	woman's son	family	8
6	*fæmnan tid*	woman's day (saint)	faith	8
7	*broþor wif*	brother's woman	family	7
8	*wifes gemana*	woman's company	body	7
9	*wifes flewsa*	woman's flux (period)	body	6
10	*wifes hus*	woman's house	other	5
11	*wifes hæmeþþing*	woman's intercourse	body	5
12	*wifes gebæru*	woman's state	other	5
13	*cyninges wif*	king's woman	family	5
14	*fæmnan lichama*	woman's body	body	5
–	other	–	–	93
–	total recurrent	–	–	210

and male, for example, *God* 'god', *man* 'man', *broþor* 'brother', *cyning* 'king', *fæder* 'father', *sunu* 'son' and *cempa* 'warrior' (cf. (33)), and in many of these the word *wif* should rather be understood as 'wife' (cf. (34)). When the female term is a modifier, the emerging pattern comprises mostly collocations with body parts and fluids, most of which are somehow related to reproduction and sexuality – that is, *meolc* 'milk', *flewsa* 'flow, period', *breost* 'breast' or *innoþ* 'womb'. The collocation *wifes meolc* appears only in OE medical texts, where human milk is a part of some medical remedies, as in (35), while other collocations, such as (36), have a more balanced corpus distribution.

(33) ond locade to þære **Godes fæmnan** hwæþer heo
 and looked to the God's woman whether she
 sceolde hine cucene þe deadne.
 would him alive or dead.
 'And (he) turned to the woman of God to check whether she wanted him alive or dead.' (comart3,Mart_5_[Kotzor]:De31,A.1.4)

(34) and sume mid oðres **mannes wife** gehæmdon;
 and some with other man's woman had intercourse
 'And some had sexual relations with another man's woman.'
 (comargaC,LS_14_[MargaretCCCC_303]:15.14.248)

(35) | gemeng | þæt | dust | wiþ | **wifes** | **meoluc** | þe
| mix | the | powder | with | woman's | milk | who
| wæpned | fede
| male child | fed

'Mix the powder with milk of a woman who fed a male child.'
(colaece,Lch_II_[3]:47.1.2.3975)

(36) | Ne | gesceop | se | ælmihtiga | God. | men | for | galnysse.
| not | made | the | almighty | God | people | for | lust
| ac | þæt | hi | gestrynon. | mid | gesceade | heora | team.
| but | that | they | beget | with | discretion | their | offspring
| and | eft | on | heora | ylde. | mid | ealle | þæt | forlæton.
| and | again | on | their | age | with | all | that | leave
| ðonne | ðæs | **wifes** | **innoð**. | unwæstmbære | bið | gehæfd
| when | the | woman's | womb | unfruitful | is | considered

'The almighty God did not create people for lust, but so that they beget their offspring with discretion and again in old age completely refrain from it when the woman's womb is considered sterile.' (cocathom2,+ACHom_II,_21:185.172.4092)

Among the recurrent collocations are also terms directly related to sexual intercourse: *wifes hæmeþþing* 'woman's intercourse', *wifes gemana* 'woman's company' and *wifes gemengness* 'woman's intercourse', illustrated in (37).

(37) | Se | ælmihtiga | fæder | gestrynde | ænne | sunu | of | him
| the | almighty | father | begot | one | son | of | him
| sylfum, | butan | **wifes** | **gemanan**
| self | without | woman's | company

'The almighty father begot a son by himself, without a woman's company.'
(coaelhom,+AHom_22:12.3295)

Figure 12 shows that 56 out of 210 (26 per cent) recurrent collocations of this type represent the pattern which might suggest possession or subordination, 'someone's (male) woman': these examples express family relations, but they clearly show that the position of the woman was inferior (with the exception of her relation to children), which agrees with the pattern revealed in the analysis of binominals. In the examples where *wif* is the modifier, the head noun never designates an adult male person. An impressive 29 per cent of collocations are related to woman's physicality, or, to be more specific, her reproductive capabilities. This, along with references to the position in the family, situates the linguistic image of the Anglo-Saxon woman in the household realm. The fact that none of the collocates in this group describes the woman's power over any aspect of her life further corroborates this observation.

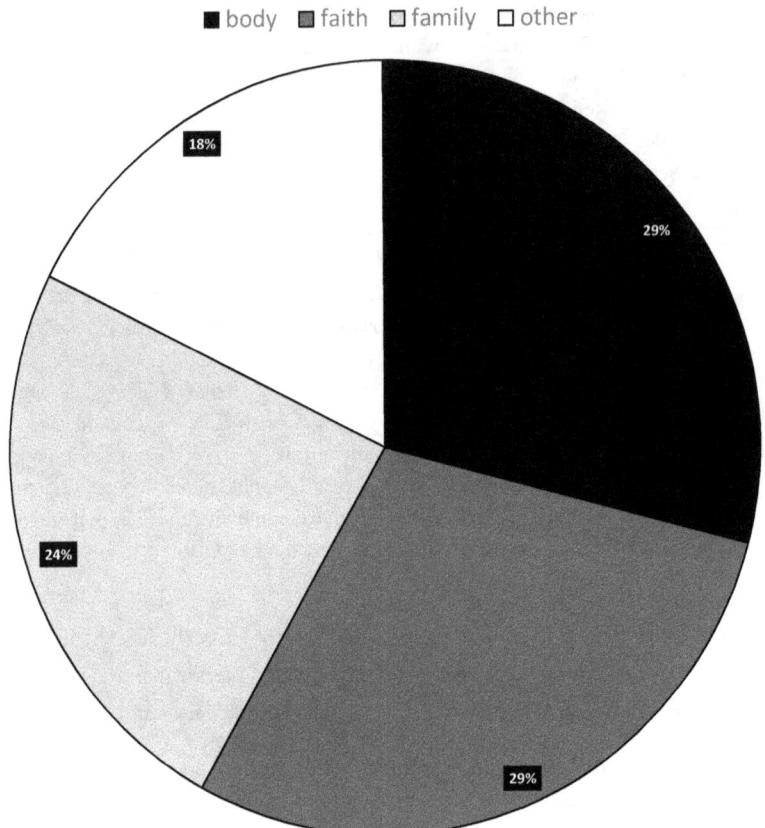

Figure 12 Genitival modification of and with *wif, fæmne* and *wifmann* 'woman' in YCOE.

In the case of *wer* 'man', the situation is drastically different, as shown in Table 17. Even though the pattern 'someone's man' is extremely well represented in the data (77 per cent of all recurrent genitival collocations), all 468 instances of such use are covered by two collocations – *Godes wer* 'God's man' and *Dryhtnes wer* 'Lord's man' – which shows that a man could only be subordinated to God, as in (38). This remarkably contrasts with genitives involving the women terms: God was merely one of the potential agents controlling a woman (namely, when she was a saint or a nun), but in other cases women were perceived as inferior to, or at least secondary to, human males.

(38) Ac þa to willan ðæs **Godes weres** heo eardiendlic wæs geworden;
but then to will the God's man she inhabitable was become
'But then, according to the will of God's man, it [the land] became inhabitable.'
(cobede,Bede_4:29.366.10.3661)

Table 17 Genitival modification of and with *wer* 'man' (> 5) in YCOE

Number	Lemma	Translation	Group	Σ
1	*Godes wer*	God's man	faith	402
2	*Dryhtnes wer*	Lord's man	faith	66
3	*lifes wer*	man of (good) life	other	25
4	*weres gemana*	man's company	body	12
5	*weres wif*	man's woman	family	9
6	*weres tid*	man's time	other	7
7	*weres wundor*	man's miracle	faith	6
8	*weres mynster*	man's monastery	faith	6
9	*weres gemynd*	man's memory	other	5
–	other	–	–	70
–	total recurrent	–	–	608

The review of genitival modification of *wer* also shows two interesting patterns absent from the collocations of the women terms. The first concerns *wer* in the position of the modifier of words such as 'time' or 'memory' – that is, nouns which generally relate to human experience. The second case concerns phrases denoting 'a man of something', where the genitival modifier of *wer* is an inanimate abstract noun such as work, holiness or life; see (39).

(39) He   sæde   me,   þæt   in   ðære   ylcan   byrig   Tudertina
      he   said   me   that   in   the   same   city   Tudertine
      wære   sum   swyþe godes **weorces** wer,   þam   wæs   nama
      was   some   very   good   work's   man   whom   was   name
      Marcellinus.
      Marcellinus
      'He told me that in the same city of Tudertine there was a man of very good work whose name was Marcellinus.' (cogregdC,GD_1_[C]:10.83.24.951)

Evidently, this collocation pattern is dominated by God's/Lord's man. This can indicate men's connection to the domain of profession and public life, since all the men of God were either future saints (and serving God was their basic activity) or members of the clergy. With only 5 per cent of collocations related to body and 1 per cent to family (cf. Figure 13), *wer* stands in stark contrast to the basic women terms, where both 'body' and 'family' cover a substantial portion of the data. Moreover, even if a man's physicality is mentioned, it is rarely related to sexuality. The only exception is *weres gemana* 'man's company', which is used in the sexual context, but all twelve cases refer to the lack of any man's physical involvement during Mary's immaculate conception as in (40).

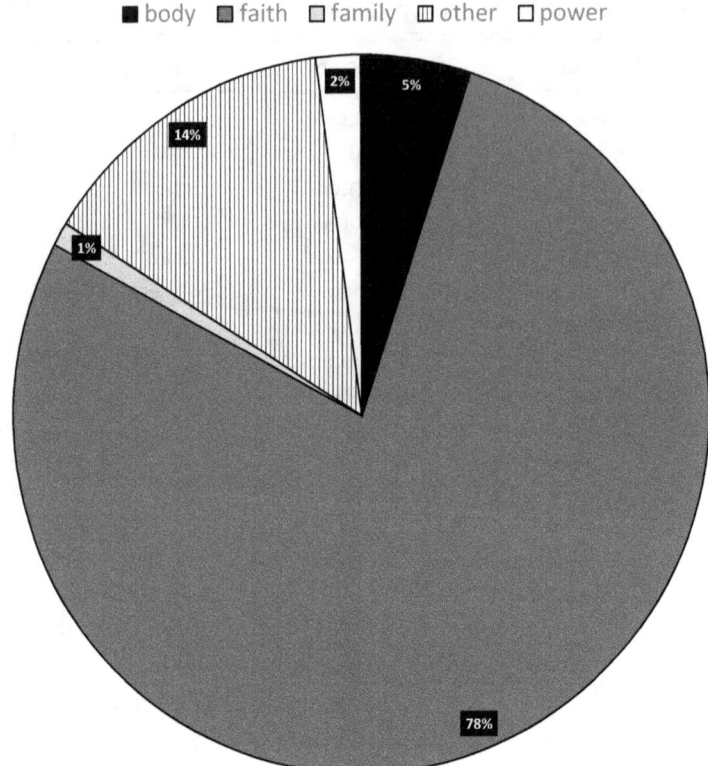

Figure 13 Genitival modification of and with *wer* 'man' in YCOE.

(40) | And | we | gelyfað | þæt | hine | clæne | mæden | gebære, | Sancta
| and | we | believe | that | him | clean | maiden | bore | Saint
| Maria, | þe | næfre | nahte | **weres** | **gemanan** | | |
| Mary | who | never | not-had | man's | company | | |

'And we believe that an immaculate maiden bore him, Saint Mary, who had never been in the company of a man.'(cowulf,WHom_7a:24.528)

The only body parts mentioned in the male context are feet and hands (cf. (41)). This markedly contrasts with the women terms, dominated in this area by *breost* 'breast' and *innoþ* 'womb.' This again stresses that bearing children was considered to be women's basic social duty, while men had a larger array of tasks to perform.

(41) | of | ðæs | **weres** | **handa** | & | his | broðor | handa | ic
| of | the | man's | hand | and | his | brother's | hand | I
| ofgange | ðæs | mannes | lif. | | | | |
| require | the | man's | life | | | | |

'I will require the life of man at the hand of every man and his brother.'(cootest, Gen:9.5.378)

Given the higher uniformity and narrower semantic scope of the analysed women terms, we can hypothesise that the linguistic image of the Anglo-Saxon man allows a more varied existence than that which is granted to the woman. Also, the category of power, though infrequent, is represented by some of the collocations. On the other hand, the linguistic patterns do not situate the Anglo-Saxon man within the domain of the family society: collocations related to family relations are rare in this group (see Figure 13).

3.3.2 Parent Terms

In the next group of terms, covering the 'parent' sense, the womb (*innoþ*) and the bosom (*bosm*) once again prove to be the most important attributes of a woman, confirming the observations related to the basic OE women terms, with (42) as a representative example.

(42) Saga   me   hwilc   sunu   wræce   ærest   his   fæder   on   hys
     tell   me   which   son   avenges   first   his   father   on   his
     moder   **innoðe**.
     mother's   womb
     'Tell me which son avenges his father already in his mother's womb.'(coadrian, Ad:12.1.31)

Table 18 shows quite clearly that similarly to the adjectival collocations, many of the patterns extracted from the corpus refer to one particular mother – that is, Mary, the mother of Jesus Christ, as in (43).

Table 18 Genitival modification of and with *modor* 'mother' (> 3) in YCOE

Number	Lemma	Translation	Group	Σ
1	hælend+modor	Saviour's mother	faith	28
2	modor+innoþ	mother's womb	body	24
3	god+modor	God's mother	faith	22
4	crist+modor	Christ's mother	faith	17
5	cyning+modor	king's mother	family	11
6	man+modor	man's mother	family	6
7	modor+bosm	mother's bosom	body	4
–	other	–	–	23
–	total recurrent	–	–	135

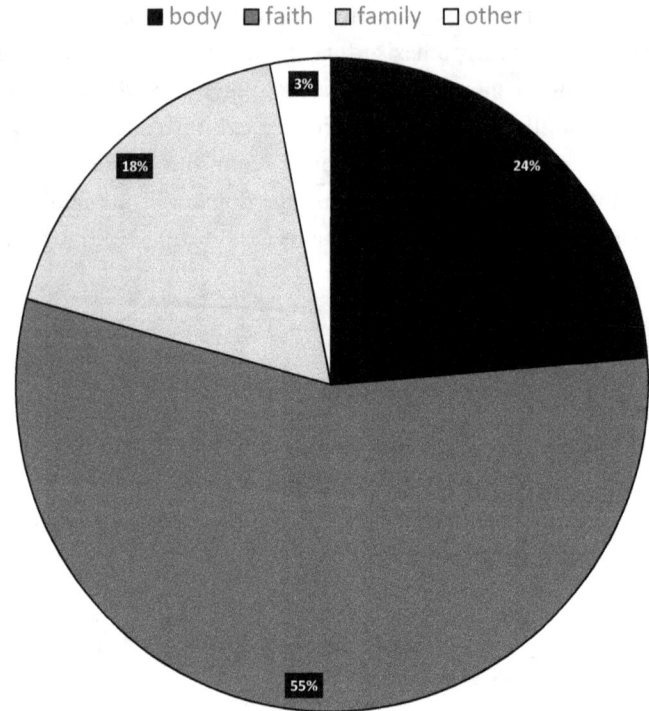

Figure 14 Genitival modification of and with *modor* 'mother' in YCOE.

(43) Ða cwæð þæs **hælendes modor** to þam þenum,
then said the Saviour's mother to the servants
doð swa hwæt swa he eow secge.
do whatever he you say
'Then the Saviour's mother said to the servants: Do whatever he tells you.'
(cowsgosp,Jn_[WSCp]:2.5.5845)

Therefore, the high proportion of 'faith', apparently at the expense of 'family', shown in Figure 14, is not surpising.

In the case of *fæder*, the data present a completely different picture. Table 19 shows that while faith remains an important category, father is mostly a modifier and often an actual or metaphorical owner of a number of objects (e.g. *hus* 'house', *æht* 'property', see (44)) and attributes (e.g. *wille* 'will, *wisdom* 'wisdom', see (45)). Example (46) shows that a father could even metaphorically 'own' his god, which is without precedence in the analysed data (a mother or a woman in general absolutely could not).

Representations of Women in Old English Prose 49

Table 19 Genitival modification of and with *fæder* 'father' (> 5) in YCOE

Number	Lemma	Translation	Group	Σ
1	fæder+god	father's God	faith	35
2	fæder+hus	father's house	family	19
3	fæder+nama	father's name	other	18
4	fæder+wille	father's will	power	15
5	fæder+rice	father's kingdom	faith	13
6	fæder+wisdom	father's wisdom	other	10
7	mynster+fæder	father of the monastery	faith	10
8	fæder+sunu	father's son	family	9
9	fæder+bysen	father's example	other	8
10	þeod+fæder	people's father	other	7
11	fæder+stefn	father's voice	body	7
12	hælend+fæder	Jesus' father	faith	6
13	fæder+æht	father's property	power	6
14	fæder+weorc	father's work	other	5
15	fæder+hiwræden	father's family	family	5
16	fæder+hand	father's hand	body	5
–	other	–	–	123
–	total recurrent	–	–	301

(44) God cwæð þa to Abrame: Far of þinum lande
God said then to Abram go of your land
& of ðinre mægðe & of ðines **fæder huse**
and of your family and of your father's house
'Then God said to Abraham: Leave your land and your family and your father's house.' (cootest,Gen:12.1.452)

(45) ac se ðe wyrcð mines **fæder willan** þe on heofonum
but this who works my father's will who on heaven
is. se færð into heofenan rice;
is this goes into heaven kingdom
'But the one who follows the will of my father, who is in heaven, goes to the kingdom of heaven.' (cocathom2,+ACHom_II,_30:235.11.5232)

(46) Ic eom þines **fæder God** & Iacobes God;
I am your father's god and Jacob's god
'I am the god of your father and the god of Jacob.' (cootest,Exod:3.6.2350)

Figure 15 shows that the data are very varied. 'Faith' is no longer a dominant category, 'power' proves to be very well represented, and while 'family' is quite important, it is clearly a minority type. Interestingly, the category 'body' proves

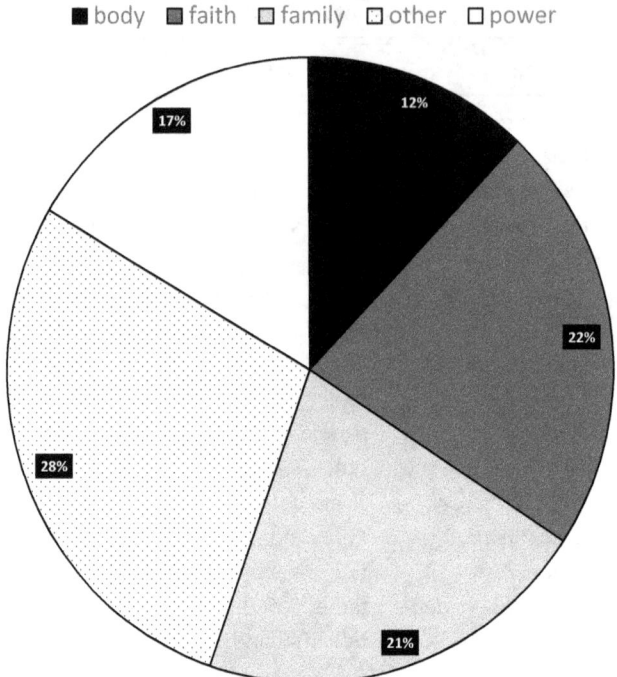

Figure 15 Genitival modification of and with *fæder* 'father' in YCOE.

rather frequent for a male term (12 per cent), but the body parts attested among the recurrent collocations are: *stefn* 'voice', *hand* 'hand', *eage* 'eye', *bosm* 'bosom', *lic* '(dead) body', *bearm* 'bosom', *fot* 'foot', *sarness* 'pain', *heorte* 'heart', *ansyn* 'face' and *bæc* 'back', so they are quite varied and rather different in character from the ones visible in women terms.

3.3.3 Terms Denoting Children and Young Adults

In the category of children and young adults, 'family' surfaces as the dominant category in the case of females. Table 20 shows how the daughters and maidens would usually belong to someone (sixty-two out of seventy-four recurrent collocations, which is 84 per cent of the data), with *innoþ* 'womb' and *nama* 'name' as the most numerous exceptions. Examples (47) and (48) illustrate the main tendencies.

(47) Mid þi ðe se cyning þas word gecwæð, ða
with this that the king these words said then
færinga þar eode in ðæs **cynges** iunge **dohtor**
suddenly there went in the king's young daughter
'When the king said these words, suddenly his young daughter came in.'
(coapollo,ApT:15.1.283)

Table 20 Genitival modification of and with *mægden* 'maiden' and *dohtor* 'daughter' (> 3) in YCOE

Number	Lemma	Translation	Group	Σ
1	cyning+dohtor	king's daughter	family	19
2	god+mægden	God's maiden	faith	16
3	ealdormann+dohtor	nobleman's daughter	family	8
4	eorl+dohtor	earl's daughter	family	4
5	broþor+dohtor	brother's daughter	family	4
6	mægden+nama	maiden's name	other	3
7	mægden+innoþ	maiden's womb	body	3
8	man+dohtor	man's daughter	family	3
–	other	–	–	14
–	total recurrent	–	–	74

(48) Se ðe   mid   deadlicum   lichaman.   Wearð   acenned
     this who with mortal   body   became   born
     of beclysedum   innoðe þæs   mædenes.
     of closed   womb   the   maiden.GEN
     'He who was born with a mortal body from the closed womb of a maiden.'
     (cocathom1,+ACHom_I,_16:308.31.2948)

As can be seen, then, 'family' proves to be the strongest category among genitival collocations (see Figure 16). For the male terms, concurrently, it is 'faith' which completely dominates the data (cf. Figure 17). The difference is driven by the fact that in many cases the referent is Jesus, *Godes sunu* 'God's son' (as shown in (49)), and this single collocation represents 61 per cent of the data in Table 21. Moreover, the second most frequent collocation, *mannes sunu* 'man's son, the son of man', is also a reference to Jesus. Nonetheless, in other cases human sons are referents, and since 95 per cent of the collocations represent the pattern 'someone's son', it suggests a subordinate position of children, which is only natural for a medieval society. The most frequent collocation in which *sunu* is the modifier is *suna lic* 'son's (dead) body' shown in (50).

(49) &   he   hyre gecydde þæt   heo scolde   geberan
     and   he   her   told   that she should   bear
     Godes sunu.
     God's son
     'And he told her that she should give birth to God's son.' (cowulf, WHom_7:38.409)

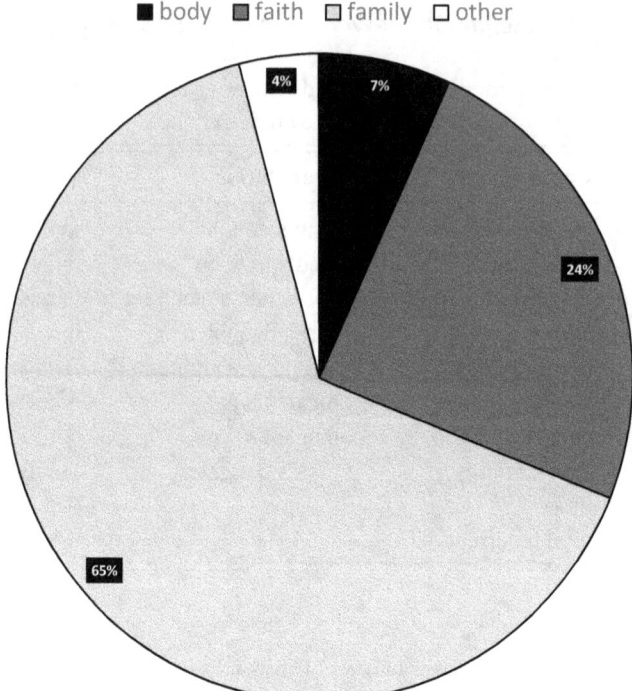

Figure 16 Genitival modification of and with *mægden* 'maiden' and *dohtor* 'daughter' in YCOE.

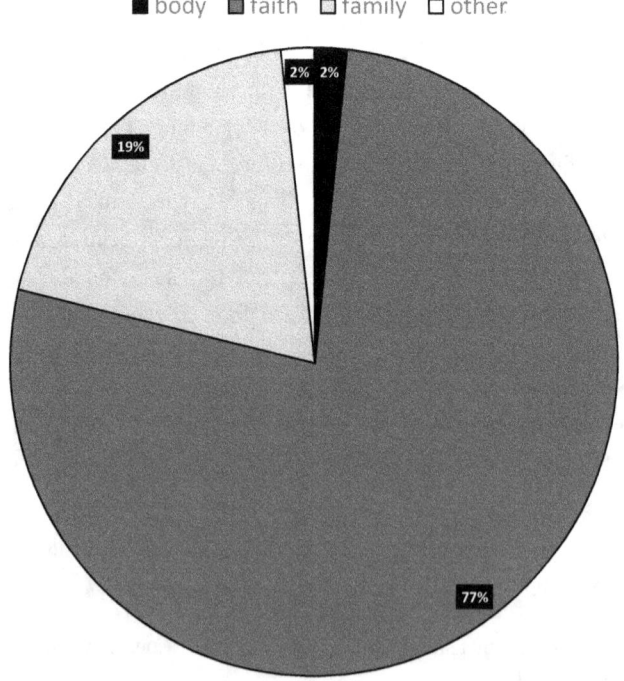

Figure 17 Genitival modification of and with *sunu* 'son' and *cnapa* 'boy' in YCOE.

Table 21 Genitival modification of and with *sunu* 'son' and *cnapa* 'boy' (> 5) in YCOE

Number	Lemma	Translation	Group	Σ
1	god+sunu	God's son	faith	434
2	man+sunu	man's son	faith	111
3	cyning+sunu	king's son	family	42
4	broþor+sunu	brother's son	family	14
5	ealdormann+sunu	nobleman's son	family	10
6	modrige+sunu	aunt's son	family	9
7	eorl+sunu	earl's son	family	9
8	sweostor+sunu	sister's son	family	8
9	wiln+sunu	maid's son	family	6
10	sunu+lic	son's body	body	5
11	sunu+sunu	son's son	family	5
12	widuwa+sunu	widow's son	family	5
13	fæder+sunu	father's son	family	5
–	other	–	–	52
–	total recurrent	–	–	715

(50) An   geleafful   yrðling   bær   his   deadan   **suna**   **lic**   to
one   religious   farmer   bore   his   dead   son's   body   to
Benedictes   mynstre.
Benedict's   monastery.
'A religious farmer brought the body of his dead son to a Benedictine monastery.' (cocathom2,+ÆCHom_II,_11:105.470.2272)

Although it has to be noted that the relatively low frequency of the collocations in this category limits their statistical relevance, they still confirm the results yielded in other categories of nouns, thus confirming a general tendency.

3.3.4 Sibling Terms

In the category 'sibling', *sweostor* 'sister' proves quite unvaried in its phraseological patterns (see Table 22). Only four recurrent genitival collocations were identified, three of which represent the semantic group of 'family', as shown in (51). The only attribute of a sister in the data is her soul, as in (52).

(51) And   Æðelswið   cwen,   seo   wæs   Ælfredes   **sweostor**
And   Aethelswith   queen   who   was   Alfred's   sister
cinges,   forðferde
king's   died
'And Aethelswith, the sister of King Alfred, died.' (cochronC,ChronC_[Rositzke]:889.1.839)

Table 22 Genitival modification of and with *sweostor* 'sister' in YCOE

Number	Lemma	Translation	Group	Σ
1	*cyning+sweostor*	king's sister	family	9
2	*sweostor+sunu*	sister's son	family	8
3	*sweostor+sawel*	sister's soul	faith	5
4	*cild+sweostor*	child's sister	family	2
–	total recurrent	–	–	24

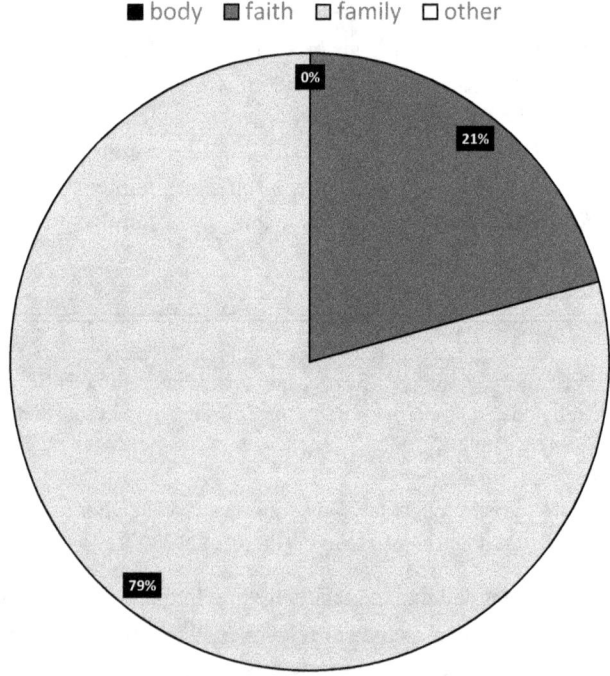

Figure 18 Genitival modification of and with *sweostor* 'sister' in YCOE.

(52) Hu   he   geseah   his   **swustor**   **sawle**,   hu   heo
     how   he   saw   his   sister's   soul   how   she
     utferde   of   lichaman.
     out-went   of   body
     'How he saw his sister's soul and how it left her body.' (cogregdH,GDHead_2_[H]:94.2.960)

Figure 18 thus diverges from the patterns attested for the previous groups of female terms, but this can be explained by the low number of collocations and their limited diversity. Consequently, this is a category of minimal relevance for our study.

Table 23 Genitival modification of and with *broþor* 'brother' (> 4) in YCOE

Number	Lemma	Translation	Group	Σ
1	cyning+broþor	king's brother	family	21
2	broþor+eage	brother's eye	body	14
3	broþor+sunu	brother's son	family	14
4	broþor+wif	brother's woman	family	7
5	mynster+broþor	brother of (the) monastery	faith	7
6	broþor+sawel	brother's soul	faith	6
7	eorl+broþor	earl's brother	family	5
8	broþor+dohtor	brother's daughter	family	4
9	broþor+gereord	brother's speech	other	4
10	broþor+þing	brother's thing	other	4
11	broþor+blod	brother's blood	body	4
–	other	–	–	50
–	total recurrent	–	–	140

In the case of *broþor* 'brother', there is both more data and more variation, as shown in Table 23. While 'family', exemplified by (53), proves to be a strong category (which is confirmed by Figure 19), it is rather unexpected that 'body' is well attested as well. This result, however, is inflated by the the high frequency of *eage* 'eye', which in turn results from numerous references of Anglo-Saxon homilies to the parable from the Gospel of Matthew: 'And why beholdest thou the mote that is in thy brother's eye, but considerest not the beam that is in thine own eye?' (cf. (54)). (The word 'brother' in this parable does not denote a family relation, but a fellow human.) The only other collocation from this category is *broþor blod* 'brother's blood', also a biblical reference, as shown in (55).

(53) Wæs   he   Cenredes   **broþor**   þæs   **cyninges**,   se   ær
     was   he   Cenred's   brother   the   king's   who   before
     him   rice   hæfde.
     him   power   had
     'He was a brother of King Cenred who ruled before him.' (cobede, Bede_5:21.476.25.4785)

(54) To   hwi   gesihst   þu   þæt   mot   on   þines   **broþor**
     to   why   see   you   the   dust   on   your   brother's
     egan
     eye
     'Why do you see the mote in your brother's eye?' (cowsgosp,Mt_[WSCp]:7.3.355)

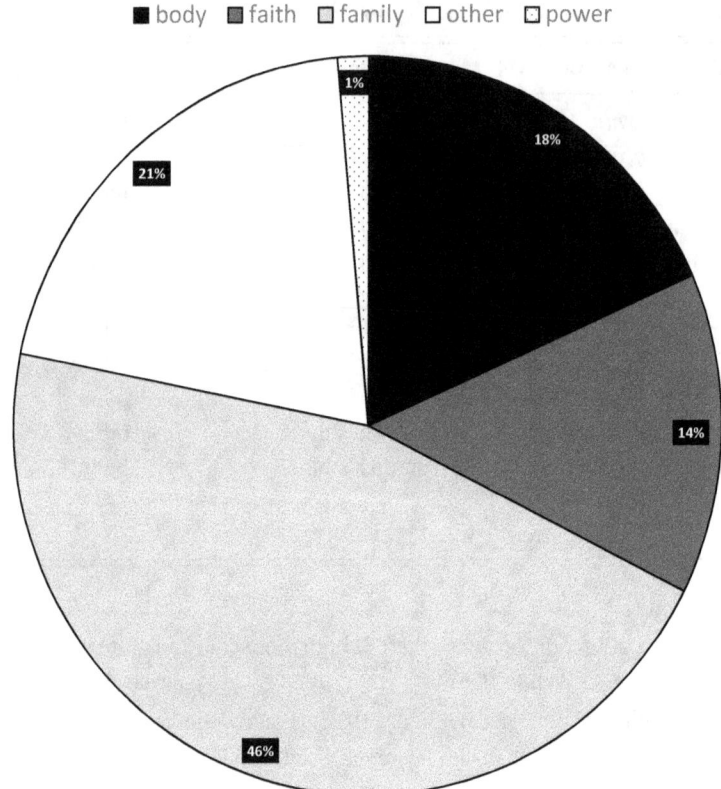

Figure 19 Genitival modification of and with *broþor* 'brother' in YCOE.

(55) þines **broðor** **blod** clypað up to me of eorðan.
 your brother's blood calls up to me of earth
 'Your brother's blood is calling me from the earth.' (cootest,Gen:4.10.189)

(56) & heo lustlice from þam **broðrum** þæs **mynstres**
 and they gladly from the brothers the monastery.GEN
 onfongne wæron.
 received were
 'And they were gladly received by the brothers of the monastery.' (cobede, Bede_3:17.234.2.2390)

Finally, it should be noted that many 'brothers' in the dataset are in fact monks, as in (56).

Analogous to the nouns describing children and young adults, the results yielded by the sibling category are not very significant statistically; however, the analysis of the collocations from this group does not deviate from a pattern visible elsewhere.

Table 24 Genitival modification of and with *cwen* 'queen', *abbodesse* 'abbess', *hlæfdige* 'lady' and *nunne* 'nun' in YCOE

Number	Lemma	Translation	Group	Σ
1	abbodesse+mynster	abbess' monastery	power	5
2	cyning+cwen	king's queen	family	4
3	mynster+abbodesse	abbess of (the) monastery	power	3
4	abbodesse+þegnung	abbess' service	power	3
5	middaneard+cwen	queen of the world	power	3
6	abbodesse+forþfor	abbess' death	other	2
7	gesamnung+abbodesse	abbess' congregation	power	2
8	god+nunne	God's nun	faith	2
9	suþdæl+cwen	queen of the south	power	2
10	yfel+cwen	queen of evil	other	2
11	þegen+cwen	servant's queen	power	2
12	god+cwen	God's queen	faith	2
13	hlæfdige+forþfor	lady's death	other	2
–	total recurrent	–	–	34

3.3.5 Terms Denoting Women and Men of High Social Status

The last group of gendered nouns, including women of higher social position, proves very interesting in its collocational choices. As in the analysis of adjectival collocations, female terms for women of an esteemed status display a strong contrast with other female nouns. Table 24 and Figure 20 convincingly show that Anglo-Saxon women of higher social standing were mostly attested in collocations related to their power and authority, for example, *abbudissan mynstre* 'abbess' monastery' in (57). However, even in the case of the woman who seems to have most power, the abbess, the data show a major limitation: while she can 'own' her monastery and her congregation, she fails to 'own' any people, unlike the men in power discussed later in this Element.

'The queen' and 'the lady' are sometimes references to Mary, the mother of Jesus, as in (58), but the queen is also often a metaphor, as in (59). This example is particularly interesting, as it provides an insight into the imagery of Christian theology. The phrase describing the hierarchic nature of cardinal sins, 'pride is the queen of all sins', is not in itself biblical. It originated in St Gregory the Great's *Moralia* (written in the late sixth century in Latin) and was later used by the Christian doctrine, for example, by Thomas Aquinas. The feminine personification of evil relies on a presupposition, convenient for male Christian

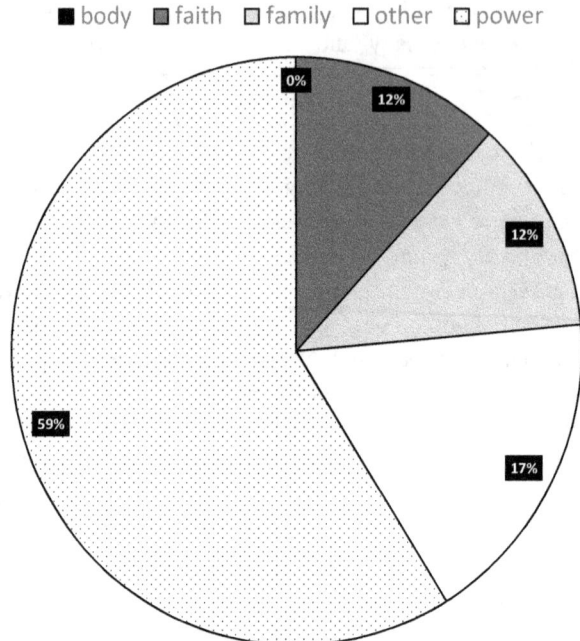

Figure 20 Genitival modification of and with *cwen* 'queen', *abbodesse* 'abbess', *hlæfdige* 'lady' and *nunne* 'nun' in YCOE.

philosophers, that all human sin is a consequence of the original sin, for which, ultimately, Eve is responsible.

(57) In ðeosse **abbudissan mynstre** wæs sum broðor syndriglice
 in this abbess' monastery was some brother particularly
 mid godcundre gife gemæred & geweorðad.
 with divine grace glorified and honoured
 'In this abbess' monastery there was a brother particularly glorified and honoured with God's grace.' (cobede,Bede_4:25.342.3.3426)

(58) Ne cwæð heo na ic eom Godes moder. oððe ic eom
 not said she not I am God's mother or I am
 cwenn ealles **middaneardes**.
 queen all world
 'She did not say: I am God's mother, or: I am the queen of all the world.'
 (cocathom1,+ACHom_I,_13:286.144.2480)

(59) Se forma heafodleahtor ys ofermodignes, Seo ys gecweden
 the first cardinal sin is pride which is said
 cwen eallra **yfela**.
 queen all.GEN evils.GEN
 'The first cardinal sin is pride, which is said to be the queen of all evils.'
 (coverhom,HomS_38_[ScraggVerc_20]:61.A.2581)

Representations of Women in Old English Prose 59

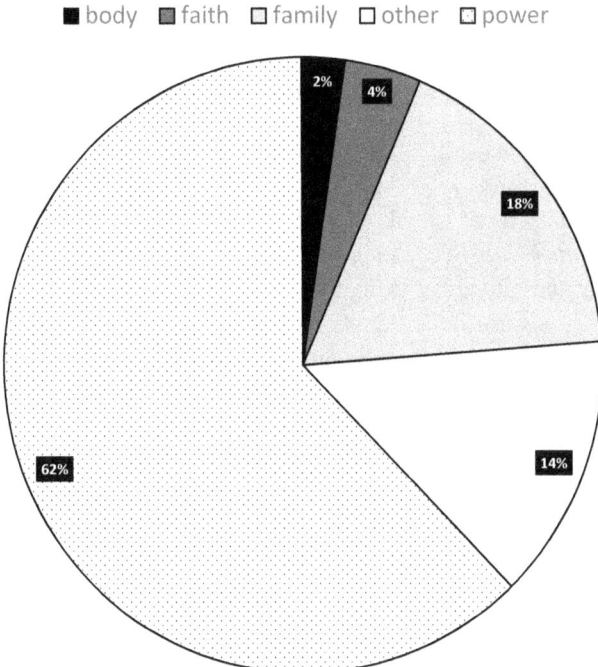

Figure 21 Genitival modification of and with *cyning* 'king', *hlaford* 'lord', *abbod* 'abbot' and *munuc* 'monk' in YCOE.

Metaphorical uses aside, Figure 20 presents a really exceptional picture, with 'power' dominant at 59 per cent, and the equivalent result for the male-gendered nouns being extremely close at 62 per cent (cf. Figure 21). Table 25 reveals, however, that while the quantitative result is virtually the same, the king's power is often expressed by the possession of servants (e.g. *cyninges þegen* 'king's servant' shown in (60) or *cyninges gerefa* king's steward').

(60) And   þa   on   ðæs   wifes   gebærum   onfundon   Þæs
     and   then   on   the   woman's   manners   found   the
     cinges þegnas   ða   unstilnesse
     king's servants   the   restlessness
     'And the king's servants found restlessness in the woman's behaviour.'
     (cochronC,ChronC_[Rositzke]:755.14.367)

It may not seem obvious why the collocation *cyninges dæg* 'king's day' was classified in the 'power' category, but, as (61) shows, it refers to the times of a king's reign, which was a way of measuring time.

Table 25 Genitival modification of and with *cyning* 'king', *hlaford* 'lord', *abbod* 'abbot' and *munuc* 'monk' (> 10) in YCOE

Number	Lemma	Translation	Group	Σ
1	cyning+þegen	king's servant	power	75
2	cyning+sunu	king's son	family	42
3	cyning+dæg	king's day(s)	power	27
4	cyning+broþor	king's brother	family	21
5	cyning+dohtor	king's daughter	family	19
6	cyning+rice	king's kingdom	power	17
7	mynster+abbod	abbot of the monastery	power	17
8	cyning+gerefa	king's steward	power	16
9	abbod+hæs	abbot's order	power	15
10	wuldor+cyning	king of glory	other	12
11	þeod+cyning	people's king	power	11
12	cyning+cyning	king of (all) kings	other	11
13	cyning+hired	king's family	family	10
–	other	–	–	541
–	total recurrent	–	–	834

(61) Hu   on   Achaie   wearþ   micel   flod   on   Ambictiones
    how   on   Achaia   became   great   flood   in   Ambiction's
    dagum þæs   **cyninges**
    days   the   king
    'How a great flood took place in Achaia in the days of King Ambiction.'
    (coorosiu,OrHead:1.6.7)

Generally, 'power' is the dominant category, and (62) is another representative example.

(62) ne   do   he   nan   ðing   butan   þæs   **abbodes**   **hæse**
    nor   do   he   no   thing   without   the   abbot's   order
    'Nor shall he do anything without the abbot's order.' (cobenrul,BenR:27.7.6.96)

The similarities between Figures 20 and 21 are quite striking and they show, as in the analysis of adjectival collocations, that the only women whose linguistic image was comparable to men's were those of a privileged social status. A higher-ranking woman was described with more positive adjectives, never associated with physicality, and the patterns of genitival modification also show that she in fact could possess some power, just like a man.

3.4 Quantitative Summary

This section is based on the analysis of a large number of recurrent collocations. In the case of adjectival modification, we took into account 576 phraseological

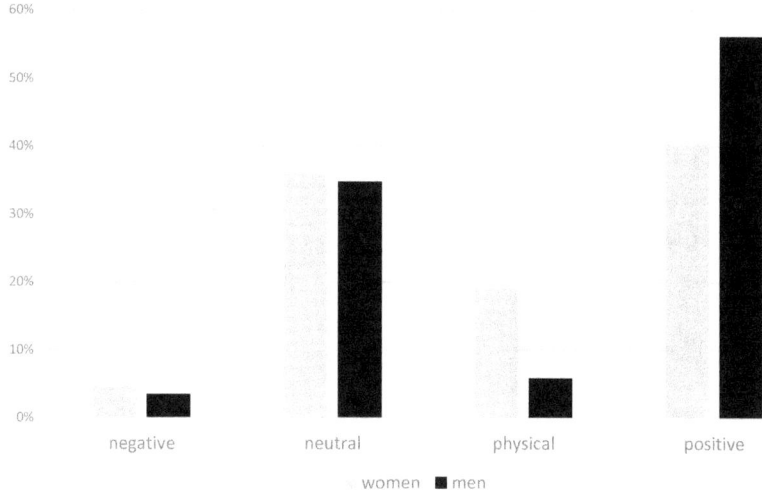

Figure 22 Adjectival modifiers of all the gendered nouns: Summary.

units with female-gendered nouns and 2,385 equivalent units with male-gendered nouns, and the proportions between the particular adjective types are illustrated by Figure 22. All in all, in turns out that while the proportions of negative and neutral adjectives for all the analysed lexemes combined are rather similar between the female and the male group, the difference in the use of adjectives related to physicality and positive features is really striking (19 per cent vs. 6 per cent and 40 per cent vs. 56 per cent respectively) and it proves statistically significant (X^2 (3, N = 2961) = 121.3653, p < 0.00001). The fact that physicality is the main factor discriminating the two groups confirms the hypothesis that female terms would rather collocate with adjectives describing physical appearance.

As far as binominals are concerned, the analysis was based on 341 units with female-gendered nouns and 468 phrases with their male equivalents. Figure 23 illustrates a few important differences that the study revealed. First of all, two female terms rarely collocate with each other (5 per cent), while binominals with two male terms are the dominant category in this group (46 per cent). Next, it is rather striking that male terms precede female terms in the majority of binominals including women (58 per cent), while only 2 per cent of the data show a reverse situation for men. The final discrepancy lies in the ability of women terms to collocate with children terms (25 per cent), and the complete lack thereof in the male dataset. The difference is confirmed by statistics: (X^2 (4, N = 809) = 556.2729, p < 0.00001) and it shows a big difference in the social position of men and women and the clear superiority of the former. At the same

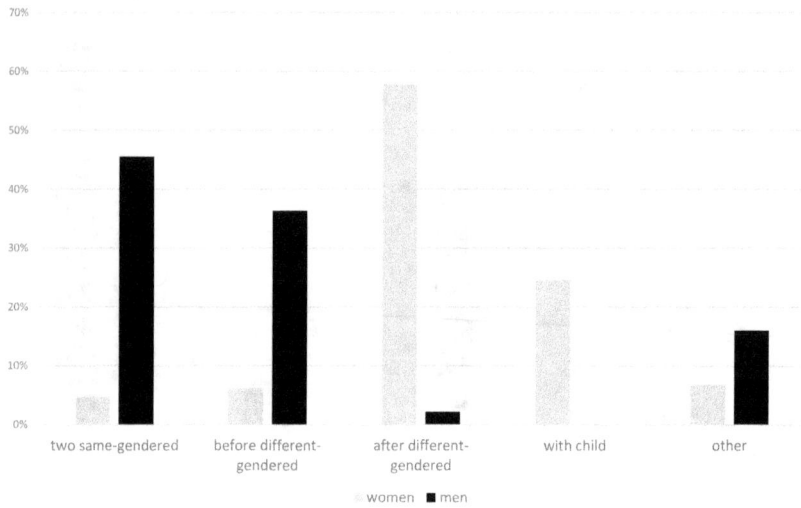

Figure 23 Binominals with all the gendered nouns: Summary.

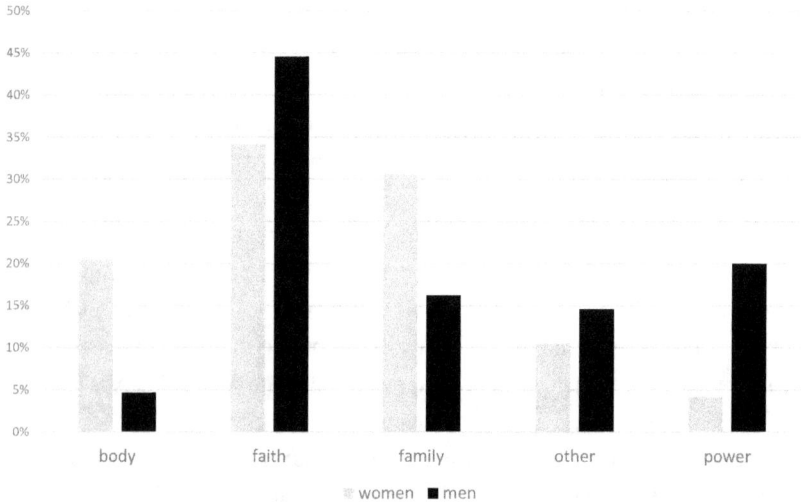

Figure 24 Genitival modification for all the gendered nouns: Summary.

time, it confirms women's close relation to family and children, reflecting their main social role.

In the case of genitival modification, the analysis covered 477 phraseological units built around women terms and 2,598 equivalent units with men terms. Figure 24 illustrates the general difference between the groups, proving that all the categories differ considerably. The most striking discrepancy is visible in collocations describing power (4 per cent for women vs. 20 per cent for men) and body (21 per cent vs. 5 per cent respectively), which are almost complete reversals of each other. The remaining differences concerning family (31 per cent for women vs. 16 per cent for men) and faith (35 per cent vs. 45 per cent respectively) complete the picture, demonstrating how Anglo-Saxon women are usually shown in term of their family relations and physicality, while men are rather portrayed against the background of their profession, which in early medieval times translates into power relations (i.e. social class and position in society) and faith (i.e. respect in the eyes of the Catholic Church). As expected, this huge difference proves statistically significant (X^2 (4, N = 3075) = 260.0851, p < 0.00001).

4 Collocations on the Level of the Verb Phrase

4.1 Subjects and Their Verbs (N + V)

4.1.1 General Terms

The next part of the analysis shows the most frequent verbs co-occurring with the analysed nouns in the syntactic role of subject. The verbs were divided into a few elementary semantic and/or syntactic categories (being, possession, activity, cognition, motion, saying, state, modal, passive), following the procedure described in Section 2, in order to show the main tendencies in the data and facilitate further analysis.

As can be seen in Table 26, in the case of general women terms, verbs of being are the most frequently represented category, which is not particularly consequential, since such verbs are generally frequent and associated with all types of subjects. Nonetheless, what does appear as rather striking is the relatively high frequency of passive structures associated with the basic women terms – that is, even though a woman is a syntactic subject, she is the patient and not the agent of the action, as in (63). In this context, it is also important to note the relatively high frequency of modal verbs, which in most cases, as illustrated by (64), refer to rules and obligations.

(63)   &   þæt   **wif**   **wæs**   **gehæled**   on   þære   tide.
       and   the   woman   was   healed   on   this   time
       'And at that time the woman was healed.' (cowsgosp,Mt_[WSCp]:9.22.553)

(64)   Se   halga   wer   þa   cwæð,   **wif**   ne   **sceal**   na   faran
       the   holy   man   then   said   woman   not   shall   not   go
       to   wera   fyrdwicum,   ac   wunian   æt   ham
       to   men's   camp   but   stay   at   home
       'Then the holy man said: A woman should not go to men's camp but stay at home.' (coaelive,+ALS_[Martin]:1095.6683)

Table 26 Verbal collocates of *wif*, *fæmne* and *wifmann* 'woman' as subjects (> 5) in YCOE

Number	Lemma	Translation	Category	Σ
1	*wif+wesan*	to be	being	46
2	*wif+cweþan*	to say	saying	12
3	*wif+beon*	to be	being	9
4	*wif+sculan*	shall	modal	8
5	*wif+weorþan*	to become	being	8
6	*fæmne+wesan*	to be	being	7
7	*wif+cennan*	to bear (a child)	activity	6
8	*wif+habban*	to have	possession	6
9	*wif+hatan*	to be called	passive	5
10	*wif+acennan*	to bear (a child)	activity	5
11	*wif+gelifan*	to believe	cognition	5
12	*wif+secgan*	to say	saying	5
13	*wif+ceorlian*	to marry	activity	5
–	other	–	–	73
–	total recurrent	–	–	200

Verbs of saying are well represented in the corpus, but this does not point to high agentivity of the analysed terms but should rather be seen as a by-product of narrative structure since numerous OE prose texts made frequent use of dialogues. However, what is important (though perhaps rather predictable at this point) is that the most frequent activity verbs collocating with *wif* are *cennan* 'to bear (a child)', *acennan* 'to bear (a child)' and *ceorlian* 'to marry', illustrated by (65), which points to a very narrow semantic range of the verbs where the woman is a true agent of the action. This is another example of limiting the Anglo-Saxon woman's activity to the family realm, ascribing to her the role of a mother and wife.

(65) To þan þæt wif cenne wæpnedcild, haran hrif gedryged
 to that that woman bears male child hare's womb dried
 & gesceafen oððe gegniden on drinc drincen
 and scraped or rubbed on drink drink
 butu.
 both

 'For a woman to bear a male child, let both [man and woman] drink dried hare's womb, scraped or rubbed into a drink.' (coquadru,Med_1.1_[de_Vriend]:5.12.200)

By contrast, the verbal collocates of *wer* are much more diverse. One of the most easily discernible differences between the male and the female terms, as

Representations of Women in Old English Prose 65

Table 27 Verbal collocates of *wer* 'man' as subject (> 5) in YCOE

Number	Lemma	Translation	Category	Σ
1	*wer*+*wesan*	to be	being	65
2	*wer*+*habban*	to have	possession	16
3	*wer*+*cweþan*	to say	saying	12
4	*wer*+*geseon*	to see	perception	10
5	*wer*+*cuman*	to come	motion	8
6	*wer*+*wunian*	to stay	motion	7
7	*wer*+*beon*	to be	being	7
8	*wer*+*feran*	to go	motion	6
9	*wer*+*andswarian*	to answer	saying	6
10	*wer*+*weorþan*	to become	being	6
11	*wer*+*gehyran*	to hear	perception	6
12	*wer*+*secgan*	to say	saying	5
–	other	–	–	118
–	total recurrent	–	–	272

shown in Table 27, is the high frequency of *habban* 'to have', which clearly indicates that possession and ownership in Anglo-Saxon society should be associated with the male gender. What is more, the activity verbs co-occurring with *wer* are, unlike for the women terms, semantically broad: various examples include *hatan* 'call/order', *don* 'to do', *locian* 'to look', *niman* 'to take', etcetera, as in (66). Some of these verbs, like *hatan*, signal not only activity but also agency and power, which certainly resides with men.

(66) ac   se   halga   **wer**   sona   **het**   hi   ætstandan,
     but   the   holy   man   soon   ordered   them   stand still
     'But the holy man soon ordered them to stand still.' (coaelive,+ALS_ [Martin]:1043.6646)

If we compare the proportions (see Figure 25), the differences between the female- and male-gendered nouns become well visible and rather substantial. In the case of *wer*, activity verbs are not only more varied but also more frequent (18 per cent vs. 14 per cent), and so are motion verbs (14 per cent vs. 8 per cent), which also indirectly relate to activity, as well as verbs of possession (7 per cent vs. 5 per cent). The verb types used more frequently with women terms are passive (9 per cent vs. 2 per cent); other verbs have comparable frequencies. All in all, this aspect of the linguistic image of Anglo-Saxons presents women as

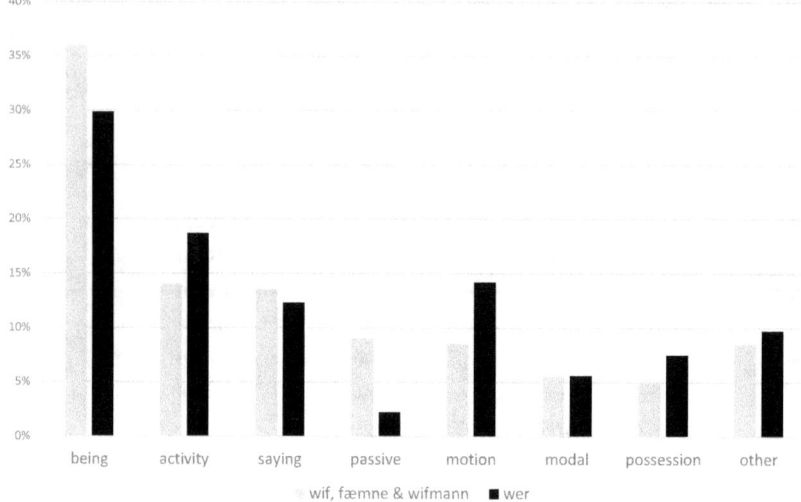

Figure 25 Verbal collocates of *wif, fæmne* and *wifmann* 'woman' vs. *wer* 'man' as subjects in YCOE.

more passive, confined to family and motherhood, whereas men are characterised as more independent participants of varied spheres of life.

4.1.2 Parent Terms

In the case of *modor* 'mother' (see Table 28), similarly to the previous group, the collocations are rarely activity verbs, and if they are, once again they are verbs related to the semantic field of childbearing, as in (67). Moreover, there is a verb related to emotions, as in (68), but these emotions are only negative (fear).

(67) geþenc þæt þe þin **modor** nacodne **gebær**.
 think that you your mother naked bore
 'Consider that when your mother gave birth to you, you were naked.'
 (codicts,Prov_1_[Cox]:1.14.24)

(68) Min **modor** ne **ondræd** þu ðe
 my mother not fear you REFL
 'Mother, do not be afraid.' (cocathom2,+ACHom_II,_42:316.188.7149)

With *fæder* 'father', the most frequent verb of emotion is clearly positive: *lufian* 'to love' as in (69).

(69) Se **fæder** **lufað** þone sunu
 the father loves the son
 'The father loves the son.' (cocathom1,+ACHom_I,_16:308.47.2963)

Representations of Women in Old English Prose 67

Table 28 Recurrent verbal collocates of *modor* 'mother' as subject in YCOE[13]

Number	Lemma	Translation	Category	Σ
1	modor+wesan	to be	being	18
2	modor+cweþan	to say	saying	4
3	modor+weorþan	to become	being	4
4	modor+beon	to be	being	3
5	modor+don	to do	activity	2
6	modor+secgan	to say	saying	2
7	modor+sittan	to sit down	motion	2
8	modor+gewitan	to understand	cognition	2
9	modor+gewunian	to stay	state	2
10	modor+gebæran	to bear (a child)	activity	2
11	modor+onbryrdan	to be inspired	passive	2
12	modor+cuman	to come	motion	2
13	modor+agan	to own	possession	2
14	modor+ondrædan	to fear	emotion	2
–	total recurrent	–	–	49

Table 29 also lists a number of collocations pertaining to (transfer of) possession, as in (70), and many activity verbs which are not limited in the same way as the women terms, which shows that men can enjoy the privilege of ownership as well as the power of agency (cf. (71)).

(70) Þa   þæt   mæden   wæs   XV   gear,   þa   wolde   se   **fæder**
     when   the   maiden   was   fifteen   years   then   would   the   father
     hi   **sellan**   sumum   æþelon   men   to   bryde.
     her   give   some   noble   man   to   bride
     'When the maiden was fifteen years old, her father wanted to give her as a bride to a nobleman.' (comart1,Mart_1_[Herzfeld-Kotzor]:De25,C.7.40)

(71) and   se   hæþene   cing   his   **fæder**   hit   **het**   ut
     and   the   heathen   king   his   father   it   ordered   out
     aweorpan
     throw
     'And his father, the heathen king, ordered to throw it out.'(comargaC,LS_14_[MargaretCCCC_303]:3.2.12)

Figure 26 summarises these tendencies, making it evident that the collocations of *fæder* show a higher proportion of (varied) activity verbs (30 per cent vs.

---

[13] The collocations of *modor* as a subject are so infrequent in the study corpus that the table shows a complete list.

Table 29 Verbal collocates of *fæder* 'father' as subject (> 5) in YCOE

Number	Lemma	Translation	Category	Σ
1	*fæder+wesan*	to be	being	102
2	*fæder+lufian*	to love	emotion	16
3	*fæder+sellan*	to give	possession	12
4	*fæder+forgyfan*	to give	possession	11
5	*fæder+habban*	to have	possession	10
6	*fæder+hatan*	to call/order	activity	10
7	*fæder+sendan*	to send	activity	8
8	*fæder+asendan*	to send	activity	7
9	*fæder+witan*	to know	cognition	6
10	*fæder+gescippan*	to make/create	activity	6
11	*fæder+ne+wesan*	to not be	being	5
12	*fæder+don*	to do	activity	5
13	*fæder+beon*	to be	being	5
–	other	–	–	126
–	total recurrent	–	–	329

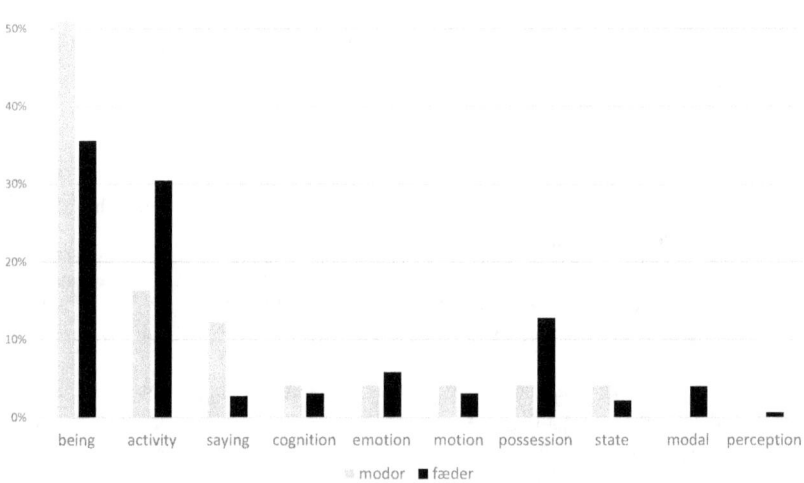

Figure 26 Verbal collocates of *modor* 'mother' vs. *fæder* 'father' as subjects in YCOE.

16 per cent) and possession (13 per cent vs. 4 per cent), while *modor* scores higher only for semantically light categories like verbs of being and saying. In this way, the results indicate similar differences in social status as those shown by the *wif/wer* category.

Table 30 Verbal collocates of *mægden* 'maiden' and *dohtor* 'daughter' as subjects (> 3) in YCOE

Number	Lemma	Translation	Category	Σ
1	*dohtor+wesan*	to be	being	21
2	*mægden+wesan*	to be	being	14
3	*mægden+cweþan*	to say	saying	9
4	*mægden+sculan*	should	modal	5
5	*mægden+geeacnian*	to conceive	activity	4
6	*mægden+arisan*	to rise	motion	3
7	*mægden+andwyrdan*	to answer	saying	3
8	*dohtor+weorþan*	to become	being	3
–	other	–	–	26
–	total recurrent	–	–	88

4.1.3 Terms Denoting Children and Young Adults

Table 30 goes to show that in the case of *mægden* 'maiden' and *dohtor* 'daughter', semantically light verbs are also dominant, and the single most frequent activity verb is, unsurprisingly at this point, *geeacnian* 'to conceive', illustrated by (72), the reference being to the Virgin Mary's immaculate conception.

(72) Efne sceal **mæden** geeacnian on hyre innoðe.
indeed shall maiden conceive on her womb
& acennan sunu.
and bear son
'Indeed, a maiden shall conceive in her womb and give birth to a son.'
(cocathom1,+ACHom_I,_13:282.25.2365)

Sunu 'son' and *cnapa* 'boy', on the other hand, show a high frequency of verbs of possession – that is, *fon* 'to take' and *habban* 'to have' shown in (73) – while the activity verbs listed in Table 31 are quite varied and include *gemiltsian* 'to take pity' and *settan* 'to set'.

(73) ond Erconberht his **sunu** feng to his rice
and Eorcenberht his son took to his power
'And his son Eorcenberht took the throne.' (cobede,Bede_3:6.172.3.1684)

Interestingly, there are also some passive uses of *sellan* 'to sell', but a closer inspection reveals that all of the instances come from the biblical story of Judas, who betrayed Jesus.

Table 31 Verbal collocates of *sunu* 'son' and *cnapa* 'boy' as subjects (> 5) in YCOE

Number	Lemma	Translation	Pattern	Σ
1	sunu+wesan	to be	being	97
2	sunu+fon	to take	possession	44
3	sunu+cuman	to come	motion	20
4	sunu+beon	to be	being	18
5	sunu+lifian	to live	state	10
6	sunu+gesellan	to be sold	passive	9
7	sunu+cweþan	to say	saying	6
8	sunu+habban	to have	possession	6
9	sunu+gemiltsian	to pity	activity	5
10	sunu+sculan	shall	modal	5
11	sunu+weorþan	to become	being	5
12	sunu+settan	to set	activity	5
13	sunu+hatan	to call	activity	5
14	sunu+sittan	to sit down	motion	5
15	sunu+don	to do	activity	5
–	other	–	–	86
–	total recurrent	–	–	331

(74) Wa þam menn þurh þone þe mannes **sunu** geseald
woe the man through whom the man's son sold
bið
is
'Woe to the man by whom man's son is sold.' (cowsgosp,Mt_[WSCp]:26.24.1862)

Figure 27 summarises these tendencies, showing that the main difference between the female and the male terms is in the use of verbs of possession (5 per cent vs. 18 per cent) and activity (9 per cent vs. 21 per cent), with the former scoring higher only for verbs of being (48 per cent vs. 39 per cent) and verbs of saying (18 per cent vs. 3 per cent).

4.1.4 Sibling Terms

In the group representing siblings, *sweostor* 'sister' proves rather poorly represented, as shown in Table 32. The only instance of an activity verb is *lætan* 'to cause, to allow' exemplified by (75); this refers to one female causing another one to do something, so it seems that the agentivity of the female referent is quite limited in this respect. As could be predicted from other patterns of agency

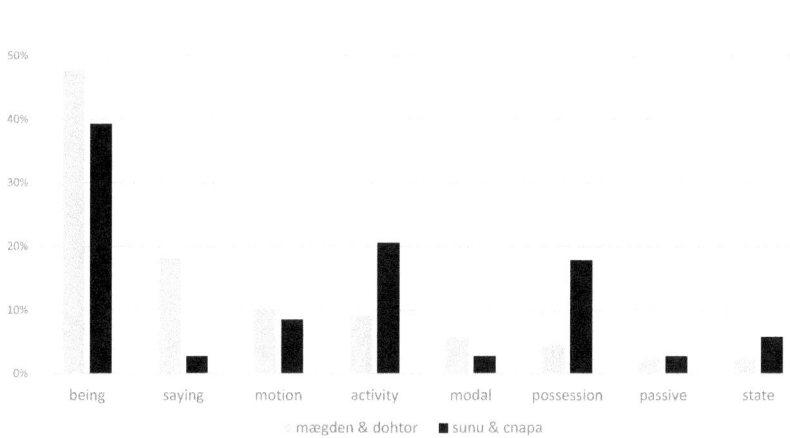

Figure 27 Verbal collocates of *mægden* 'maiden' and *dohtor* 'daughter' vs. *sunu* 'son' and *cnapa* 'boy' as subjects in YCOE.

Table 32 Verbal collocates of *sweostor* 'sister' as subject in YCOE

Number	Lemma	Translation	Pattern	Σ
1	*sweostor+wesan*	to be	being	9
2	*sweostor+lætan*	to cause/allow	activity	3
3	*sweostor+gan*	to go	motion	2
–	total recurrent	–	–	14

in Anglo-Saxon society, there are no examples showing that a woman is empowered to cause a man to do something.

(75) & cwæþ, Drihten, nis þe nan caru þæt min
 and said Lord not-is you no care that my
 swustur let me ænlipie þenian
 sister caused me alone serve
 'And said: Lord, don't you care that my sister made me serve on my own.'
 (cowsgosp,Lk_[WSCp]:10.40.4533)

Table 33 shows how *broþor* 'brother' diverges from this picture, mostly by its frequent co-ocurrence with verbs of possession – that is, *fon* 'to take' and *habban* 'to have', illustrated in (76).

Table 33 Verbal collocates of *broþor* 'brother' as subject (> 5) in YCOE

Number	Lemma	Translation	Pattern	Σ
1	broþor+wesan	to be	being	39
2	broþor+fon	to take	possession	18
3	broþor+beon	to be	being	11
4	broþor+cuman	to come	motion	10
5	broþor+habban	to have	possession	8
6	broþor+don	to do	activity	7
7	broþor+forþferan	to die	state	6
8	broþor+faran	to go	motion	6
9	broþor+cweþan	to say	saying	5
–	other	–	–	62
–	total recurrent	–	–	172

(76) Hu   Domitianus, Tituses **broðor**, **feng** to   Romano
     how   Domitian   Titus'   brother   took   to   Roman
     anwalde.
     power
     'How Domitian, the brother of Titus, took the Roman throne' (coorosiu, OrHead:6.9.70)

The most frequent activity verb is the semantically broad but clearly agentive *don* 'to do', illustrated in (77).

(77) Eala   ðu   man   þu   sceawast   hwæt   þin   **broðer**
     alas   you   man   you   show   what   your   brother
     ðe   **dyde**.
     you   did
     'Alas, man, you have shown what your brother has done to you.' (cocathom1, +ACHom_I,_3:204.169.605)

Figure 28 suggests an enourmous discrepancy between *sweostor* 'sister' and *broþor* 'brother', but this stems mostly from a quantity difference which translates directly into small diversity of the former. Consequently, this category does not yield very useful results.

4.1.5 Terms Denoting Women and Men of High Social Status

Finally, in the category of higher social status, for the first time in this section, we see frequent recurrent uses of verbs of possession with women terms – that is, *habban* 'to have' and *fon* 'to take' (see Table 34) – though a closer inspection of examples such as (78) reveals that the objects owned

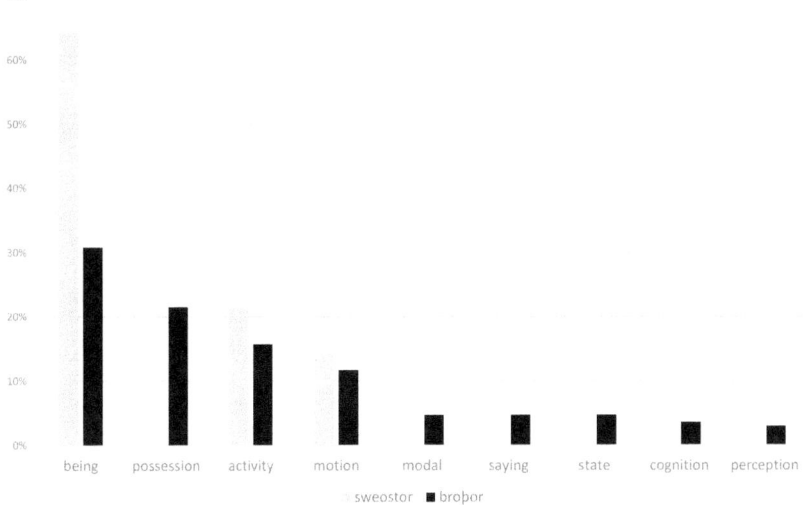

Figure 28 Verbal collocates of *sweostor* 'sister' vs. *broþor* 'brother' as subjects in YCOE.

or taken by the women were not necessarily tangible, unlike with men. However, example (79) is one of the rare occasions that describes a woman taking control over a kingdom, unusual as the story must have sounded to an Anglo-Saxon reader.

(78) Seo **cwen** **hæfde** getacnunge þære halgan gelaðunge
 the queen had warning signals the holy congregation
 ealles cristenes folces
 all Christian folk
 'The queen had some warning signs about the holy congregation of all Christians.' (cocathom2,+ACHom_II,_45:340.172.7642)

(79) & æfter his deaðe Sameramis his **cwen** **fengc** ægþer
 and after his death Semeramis his queen took either
 ge to þæm gewinne ge to þæm rice.
 and to the war and to the kigdom
 'And after his death, Semeramis replaced him as the head of the army and the ruler of the kingdom.' (coorosiu,Or_1:2.22.8.437)

Moreover, even though *faran* 'to go', a verb signalling active movement, features as one of the most frequent collocations, it turns out that in all of the examples the women do not travel on their own, but rather accompanied by men as in (80).

Table 34 Verbal collocates of *cwen* 'queen', *abbodesse* 'abbess', *hlæfdige* 'lady' and *nunne* 'nun' as subjects in YCOE

Number	Lemma	Translation	Pattern	Σ
1	cwen+wesan	to be	being	4
2	cwen+feran	to travel	motion	4
3	cwen+weorþan	to become	being	3
4	cwen+habban	to have	possession	2
5	cwen+fon	to take	possession	2
6	cwen+arisan	to rise	motion	2
7	abbodesse+wesan	to be	being	5
8	nunne+wesan	to be	being	2
9	nunne+libban	to live	state	2
10	nunne+weorþan	to become	being	2
–	total recurrent	–	–	28

(80) Her   Forðhere   bisceop   and   Friþogyð   **cwen**   **ferdon**
here   Forthhere   bishop   and   Frithogith queen   went
to   Rome.
to   Rome
'Then Bishop Forthhere and Queen Frithogith went to Rome.' (cochronC, ChronC_[Rositzke]:737.1.326)

For the equivalent male terms, a great number and variation of collocations was identified in the corpus, as evidenced by Table 35. While the abundance of activity verbs such as *hatan* 'to call, to order' shown in (81) and verbs of possession patterns with our previous observations regarding male-gendered nouns, it should be noted that in this group there is also a high number of (change of) state verbs such as *forþferan* 'to die' shown in (82) and passive constructions, with numerous chronicle entries reporting the death of a king, such as (83).

(81) In   þære ceastre eac swylce Æðelberht   **cyning** **heht**   cirican
in   this town   also   Aethelberht king   ordered   church
getimbran   &   þa   gehalgian   Sancte   Andreæ   þæm
build   and   this   consecrate St.   Andrew   the
apostoli.
apostle
'Moreover, in the same town King Aethelberht ordered a church to be built and consecrated to St. Andrew the apostle.' (cobede,Bede_2:3.104.21.983)

Table 35 Verbal collocates of *cyning* 'king', *hlaford* 'lord', *abbod* 'abbot' and *munuc* 'monk' as subjects (> 10) in YCOE

Number	Lemma	Translation	Pattern	Σ
1	cyning+wesan	to be	being	129
2	cyning+forþferan	to die	state	103
3	cyning+ofslean	to be killed	passive	61
4	cyning+cuman	to come	motion	36
5	cyning+habban	to have	possession	32
6	cyning+hatan	to order/call	activity	31
7	cyning+sendan	to send	activity	29
8	cyning+gyfan	to give	possession	24
9	cyning+faran	to go	motion	20
10	cyning+gefeohtan	to fight	activity	20
11	munuc+wesan	to be	being	19
12	hlaford+wesan	to be	being	17
13	cyning+sellan	to give	possession	16
14	cyning+weorþan	to become	being	16
15	cyning+onfon	to take	possession	16
16	cyning+fon	to take	possession	15
17	cyning+oferhergian	to ravage	activity	14
18	abbod+forþferan	to die	state	14
19	cyning+willan	to want	modal	13
20	cyning+lætan	to let	activity	12
21	cyning+niman	to take	possession	12
22	cyning+cweþan	to say	saying	12
23	cyning+beon	to be	being	11
24	cyning+gewendan	to turn	motion	10
25	cyning+feran	to go	motion	10
26	cyning+sculan	shall	modal	10
27	cyning+gan	to go	motion	10
–	other	–	–	489
–	total recurrent	–	–	1,201

(82) Her   Cuþred   Westseaxna   **cyning**   forðferde
     here   Cuthred   West Saxon   king   died
     'Then Cuthred, the king of Wessex, died.' (cochronD,ChronD_[Classen-Harm]
     :754.1.200)

(83) Her   Anna   **cining**   werð   **ofslagen**.
     here   Anna   king   became   killed
     'Then King Anna was killed.' (cochronE,ChronE_[Plummer]:653.1.365)

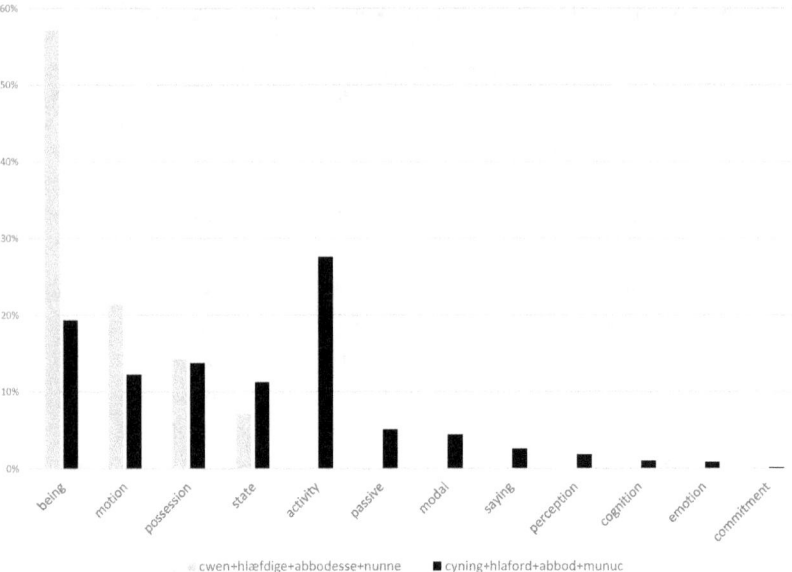

Figure 29 Verbal collocates of *cwen* 'queen', *abbodesse* 'abbess', *hlæfdige* 'lady' and *nunne* 'nun' vs. verbal collocates of *cyning* 'king', *hlaford* 'lord', *abbod* 'abbot' and *munuc* 'monk' as subjects in YCOE.

Figure 29 shows that despite the lower number of collocations attested for women terms, it is possible to observe that in this group of nouns, verbs of possession fail to drive the difference between the male and the female (both featuring *c.* 14 per cent of these verbs), and the main discrepancy lies in the complete lack of activity verbs with women terms (and 27 per cent of them for the men terms).

4.2 Objects and Their Verbs (V + N)

4.2.1 General Terms

The last collocation pattern involves the use of gendered nouns as objects. Table 36 shows quite evidently that in the case of the basic OE women terms, the predominant semantic category is possession, which clearly agrees with the masculinist perception of a woman as a material object that can be owned and transferred.

Table 36 Verbal collocates with *wif*, *fæmne* and *wifmann* 'woman' as subjects (> 3) in YCOE

Number	Lemma	Translation	Category	Σ
1	habban+wif	to have a woman	possession	46
2	niman+wif	to take a woman	possession	21
3	forlætan+wif	to leave a woman	motion	16
4	geniman+wif	to take a woman	possession	16
5	brucan+wif	to use a woman	activity	7
6	sellan+wif	to give a woman	possession	7
7	geniman+fæmne	to take a woman	possession	6
8	befæstan+wif	to secure a woman	possession	5
9	onfon+wif	to take (to) wife	possession	5
10	geseon+wif	to see a woman	perception	4
11	gelædan+wif	to lead a woman	activity	4
12	cweþan+wif	to say to a woman	saying	4
13	forgyfan+wif	to give a wife	possession	4
14	lædan+wif	to lead a woman	activity	4
15	feccan+wif	to fetch a woman	possession	3
16	beweddian+wif	to wed a woman	activity	3
17	gehælan+wif	to heal a woman	activity	3
–	other	–	–	40
–	total recurrent	–	–	198

(84) Moyses   us   wrat   gif   hwæs broðor byð dead   &   **wif**
     Moses   us   wrote if   whose brother is dead and woman
     hæbbe, & se   byð butan   bearnum   þæt his   broðor
     has   and this is without children   that his   brother
     nime his **wif** & hys   broþor   sæd awecce.
     take   his wife   and his brother's   seed awake
     'Moses wrote: if someone's brother is dead and he has a woman and no children, his brother should take his wife and awaken his brother's seed.' (cowsgosp,Mk_[WSCp]:12.19.3144)

As far as *wer* is concerned, the most interesting fact about the verb–object collocations is that they are hardly attested (see Table 37). The most common one is *geceosan* 'to choose' shown in (85).

(85) Þu   hafast **gecoren** þone **wer** þe   me   wel   licað.
     you   have   chosen   the   man   that me   well likes
     'You have chosen a man whom I like.' (coapollo,ApT:22.13.473)

Another example, *habban wer* 'to have a man', shown in (86), is attested but much less frequent than *habban wife* 'to have a woman'. Interestingly, among

Table 37 Verbal collocates with *wer* 'man' as object (> 3) in YCOE

Number	Lemma	Translation	Category	Σ
1	geceosan+wer	to choose a man	activity	10
2	habban+wer	to have a man	possession	7
3	onfon+wer	to take a man	possession	5
4	brucan+wer	to defile a man	activity	5
5	gyldan+wer	to pay a man	advantage	5
6	ofslean+wer	to kill a man	activity	5
7	sellan+wer	to give to a man	advantage	4
8	forlætan+wer	to leave a man	motion	3
9	gehyran+wer	to hear a man	perception	3
10	abidan+wer	to await a man	activity	3
–	other	–	–	16
–	total recurrent	–	–	66

the most frequent collocates there is *brucan weres* 'to enjoy a man', which appears in a clearly sexual context, which is also as a reference to a biblical story (cf. (87)).

(86) And gif hwylc geleafful wif **hæfð** ungeleaffulne **wer**, and
 and if some faithful woman has unfaithful man and
 he wylle wunian mid hyre, ne forlæte heo hine;
 he will stay with her, not leave she him
 'And if a faithful wife has an unfaithful husband and he wants to stay with her, she should not leave him.' (coaelhom,+AHom_20:97.2982)

(87) Ða andwyrde Maria þam engle. Hu mæg þis gewurðan:
 then answered Mary the angel how may this become
 for ðan þe Ic ne **bruce** nanes **weres**?
 because I not enjoyed no man
 'Then Mary answered the angel: How can this be since I have not known any man?' (cocathom1,+ACHom_I,_13:283.55.2402)

Figure 30 illustrates the difference between female and male gendered nouns in this respect. When we compare these results to the ones shown in the preceding section, it turns out that *wer* appears in recurrent collocations as subject in 15.7 per cent out of its 1,732 uses in YCOE and as object in only 3.8 per cent of its uses. The respective results for the most frequent woman term, *wif*, are 12.5 per cent as subject and 13.2 per cent as object, which is a huge discrepancy pointing to the conceptual and consequently linguistic objectification of *wif* (and women in general) in the OE prose records. The prototypical semantic role of a syntactic subject is agent: an animate and volitional doer of the action, while for

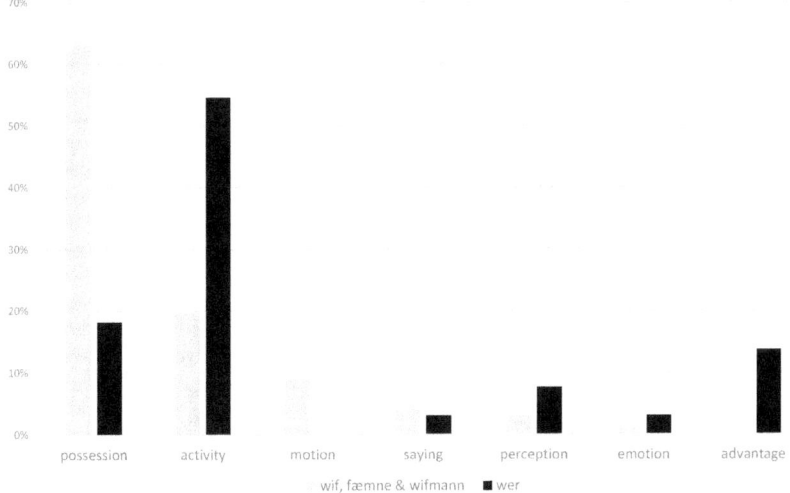

Figure 30 Verbal collocates of *wif*, *fæmne* and *wifmann* 'woman' vs. verbal collocates of *wer* 'man' as objects in YCOE.

a syntactic object it is patient: an entity (not necessarily animate) undergoing the action. Since the fact that male-gendered phrases are more likely to be syntactic subjects is generally treated as an example of gender bias in many languages, including English (e.g. Kotek et al. 2020), it is plausible to assume that the discrepancy in the proportions of subjects and objects between *wif* and *wer* in OE may be a linguistic marker of the social objectification of women in Anglo-Saxon society.

4.2.2 Parent Terms

In the case of *modor*, because of its lower frequency, the collocations are not particularly varied (see Table 38). Example (88) illustrates one of the most frequent ones.

(88) Eall þis tacnode   þæt   seo   clæne fæmne cende sunu,
     all this meant   that   the   clean woman bore son
     swa hire næfre wer   ne gehran,   ac   se   ðe
     as   her never man   not touched   but   this who
     hæfde fæder on   heofnum   butan meder and **hæfde** þa
     had   father on   heavens   without mother and had   the
     modur on   eorðan butan fæder.
     mother on   earth without father
     'All this meant that the immaculate woman gave birth to a son, even though no man had ever touched her, and he had a father in heaven without a mother, and a mother on earth without a father.' (comart1,Mart_1_[Herzfeld-Kotzor]:De25, A.28.20)

Table 38 Recurrent verbal collocates with *modor* 'mother' as object in YCOE

Number	Lemma	Translation	Category	Σ
1	habban+modor	to have a mother	possession	3
2	betæcan+modor	to entrust a mother	activity	3
3	gelædan+modor	to lead a mother	motion	2
4	geceosan+modor	to choose (for) a mother	activity	2
–	total recurrent	–	–	10

Table 39 Verbal collocates with *fæder* 'father' as object (> 5) in YCOE

Number	Lemma	Translation	Category	Σ
1	habban+fæder	to have a father	possession	14
2	swerian+fæder	to promise a father	commitment	12
3	gehyran+fæder	to hear a father	perception	10
4	arwurþian+fæder	to honour a father	activity	7
5	lufian+fæder	to love a father	emotion	7
6	biddan+fæder	to ask a father	saying	7
7	bebyrgan+fæder	to bury a father	activity	6
8	forlætan+fæder	to leave a father	motion	5
9	secgan+fæder	to tell a father	saying	5
10	gebletsian+fæder	to bless a father	activity	5
11	behatan+fæder	to promise a father	commitment	5
12	weorþian+fæder	to honour a father	activity	5
–	other	–	–	81
–	total recurrent	–	–	169

Interestingly, the YCOE data suggest that one can actually choose a mother, though a closer analysis of the examples revealed that this activity was limited to Christ (cf. (89)).

(89) Ure   Hælend   Crist   cydde,   þæt   he   lufode   þa   clænnysse
    our   saviour   Christ   said   that   he   loved   the   cleanliness
    on   his   þeowum   swutelice, þa   þa   he   mædenmann
    on   his   servants clearly   then   when he   maiden
    him   **to   meder   geceas**.
    him   to   mother   chose
    'Our Saviour Christ clearly showed that he loved cleanliness in his servants when he chose a maiden for his mother.' (colsigef,+ALet_5_[Sigefyrth]:13.7)

The collocations featuring *fæder* 'father' as an object are, in contrast, quite varied (see Table 39). Apart from the fact than one can simply 'have' a father, there are also two verbs of commitment here: *swerian* 'to swear, to promise' shown in (90) and *behatan* 'to promise', which can be interpreted as a sign of the higher authority of the father. Moreover, there is also *arwurþian* 'to honour' illustrated in (91), or *gebletsian* 'to bless'; no verbs of this type appear for *modor* 'mother', which is rather surprising, especially because this category includes the mother of Jesus.

(90) ne he ne   forgyt   his wedd, on ðam he **swor**
     nor he not forgot   his wed   on that he swore
     eowrum **fæderum**.
     you.DAT fathers.DAT
     'Nor did he forget his wed that he swore to your fathers,' (cootest,Deut:4.30.4561)

(91) Ac   ic **arwurðie** minne **fæder**.
     but I   honour   my   father
     'But I honour my father' (cocathom2,+ACHom_II,_13:128.21.2786)

Figure 31 suggests a very strong difference between *modor* 'mother' and *fæder* 'father' in their use as objects, but it is necessary to remember that the low frequency of collocations with the former term makes this graph rather difficult to interpret.

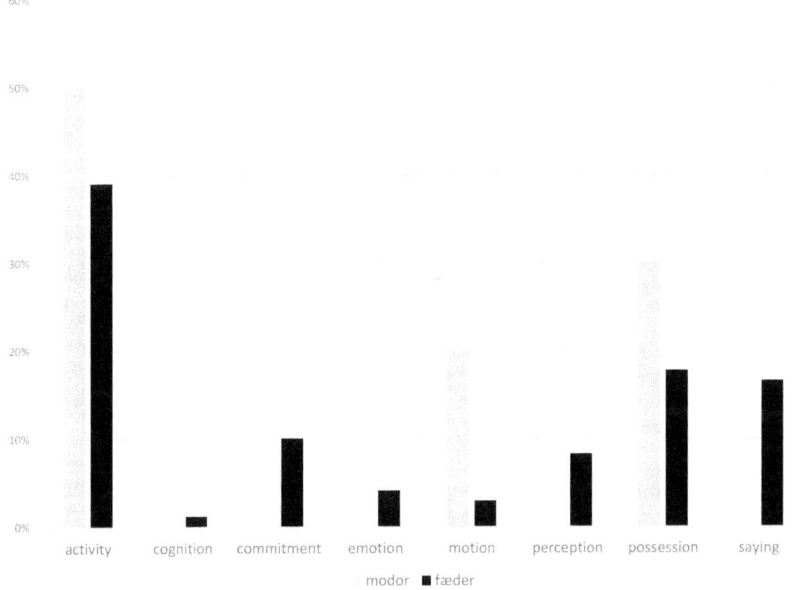

Figure 31 Verbal collocates of *modor* 'mother' vs. *fæder* 'father' as objects in YCOE.

Table 40 Verbal collocates with *mægden* 'maiden' and *dohtor* 'daughter' as object in YCOE

Number	Lemma	Translation	Category	Σ
1	habban+dohtor	to have a daughter	possession	15
2	sellan+dohtor	to give a daughter	possession	4
3	onfon+mægden	to take a maiden	possession	3
4	geseon+mægden	to see a maiden	perception	3
5	aræran+mægden	to raise a maiden	activity	2
6	gehelan+mægden	to heal a maiden	activity	2
7	underfon+dohtor	to take a daughter	possession	2
8	biddan+dohtor	to ask a daughter	saying	2
9	onfon+dohtor	to take a daughter	possession	2
10	lætan+dohtor	to let a daughter	activity	2
11	forgyfan+dohtor	to give a daughter	possession	2
12	gestrynan+dohtor	to beget a daughter	activity	2
13	befæstan+dohtor	to secure a daughter	activity	2
14	gyfan+dohtor	to give a daughter	possession	2
–	total recurrent	–	–	45

4.2.3 Terms Denoting Children and Young Adults

In the category of children and young adults (see Table 40), *mægden* 'maiden' and *dohtor* 'daughter' seem dominated by verbs of possession such as *habban* 'to have', *sellan* 'to give, to sell', as shown in (92) and *onfon* 'take', illustrated by (93).

(92) Laban **hæfde** twa **dohtra**;
Laban had two daughters
'Laban had two daughters.' (cootest,Gen:29.16.1196)

(93) Arues wende þæt he his rice gemiclian sceolde
Arues thought that he his kingdom enlarge should
þa he his **dohtor** Philippuse **sealde**.
when he his daughter Phillippus.DAT gave
'Arues thought that it would enlarge his kingdom if he gave his daughter to Philippus.' (coorosiu,Or_3:7.62.2.1186)

Interestingly, Table 41 shows that verbs of possession are also quite frequent for *sunu* 'son' and *cnapa* 'boy' – that is, *habban* 'to have' shown in (94) and *sellan* 'to give, to sell' in (95) – but there is also a number of activity verbs, mostly from the semantic field of conception and childbearing such as *gestrynan* 'to beget' shown in (96), *acennan* 'to bear' and *cennan* 'to bear'.

Representations of Women in Old English Prose 83

Table 41 Verbal collocates with *sunu* 'son' and *cnapa* 'boy' as object (> 4) in YCOE

Number	Lemma	Translation	Pattern	Σ
1	habban+sunu	to have a son	possession	33
2	gestrynan+sunu	to beget a son	activity	29
3	acennan+sunu	to bear a son	activity	20
4	cennan+sunu	to bear a son	activity	8
5	sellan+sunu	to give a son	possession	7
6	geseon+sunu	to see a son	perception	7
7	underfon+cnapa	to take a boy	possession	7
8	asendan+sunu	to send a son	activity	6
9	gehealan+cnapa	to heal a boy	activity	5
10	ofslean+sunu	to kill a son	activity	4
11	brengan+sunu	to bring a son	activity	4
12	sendan+sunu	to send a son	activity	4
13	lufian+sunu	to love a son	activity	4
14	aræran+sunu	to raise a son	activity	4
15	forlætan+sunu	to leave a son	motion	4
–	other	–	–	49
–	total recurrent	–	–	195

(94) Abraham,   ðe   heahfæder,   **hæfde**   twægen   **sunu**,
     Abraham   the   high-father   had   two   sons
     Ismael &   Isaac,
     Ismeal and Isaac
     'Abraham the patriarch has two sons, Ismael and Isaac.' (colsigewB,+ALet_4_[SigeweardB]:247.57)

(95) Drihten   me   **sealde**   ðisne   **sunu**   for   Abel,   ðe   Cain
     Lord   me   gave   this   son   for   Abel   whom   Cain
     ofsloh.
     killed
     'Lord gave me this son for Abel, who was killed by Cain.' (cootest,Gen:4.25.219)

(96) Eft   Adam   **gestrynde**   **sunu**   ðone   he   nemde   Seth,
     again   Adam   begot   son   whom   he   named   Seth
     'Again Adam begot a son, whom he named Seth.' (cootest,Gen:4.25.217)

Nevertheless, when proportions are counted (cf. Figure 32), verbs of possession turn out to be much more frequent for the female terms (67 per cent vs. 27 per cent). A noticeable frequency of those verbs in the male part of this category can be certainly explained by the lower status of younger males in

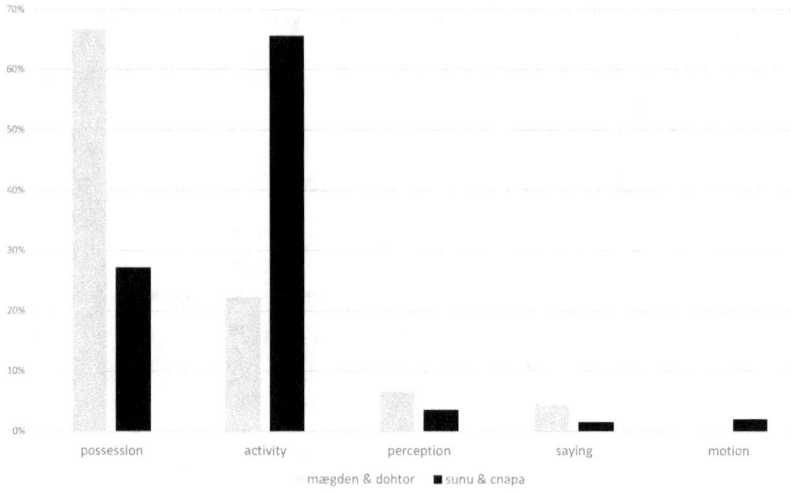

Figure 32 Verbal collocates of *mægden* 'maiden' and *dohtor* 'daughter' vs. *sunu* 'son' and *cnapa* 'boy' as objects in YCOE.

comparison with adult Anglo-Saxon men represented by the male-gendered general term *wer*.

4.2.4 Sibling Terms

In the next group of nouns, collocations with the female term *sweostor* 'sister' prove quite infrequent (see Table 42), though the recurrent ones follow the already identified patterns: possession, as in (97) and activity centred around marriage, as in (98).

(97) And he **geaf** his **sweostor** ofer sæ Ealdseaxna
 and he gave his sister over sea Old Saxon
 cynges suna.
 king's son
 'And he gave his sister away over the see to the king of the Old Saxons.'
 (cochronD,ChronD_[Classen-Harm]:924.5.1052)

Table 42 Verbal collocates with *sweostor* 'sister' as object in YCOE

Number	Lemma	Translation	Pattern	Σ
1	*habban+sweostor*	to have a sister	possession	4
2	*anforlætan+sweostor*	to leave a sister	motion	2
3	*gewifian+on+sweostor*	to marry a sister	activity	2
4	*gyfan+sweostor*	to give a sister	possession	2
–	total recurrent	–	–	10

Table 43 Verbal collocates with *broþor* 'brother' as object in YCOE

Number	Lemma	Translation	Pattern	Σ
1	secgan+broþor	to tell a brother	saying	11
2	ofslean+broþor	to kill a brother	activity	8
3	habban+broþor	to have a brother	possession	8
4	cyþan+broþor	to tell a brother	saying	5
5	sendan+broþor	to send a brother	activity	5
6	sellan+broþor	to give a brother	possession	4
7	biddan+broþor	to ask a brother	saying	4
8	gecigan+broþor	to call a brother	activity	4
9	niman+broþor	to take a brother	possession	4
10	healdan+broþor	to hold a brother	possession	3
11	adrifan+broþor	to drive away a brother	motion	3
12	reccan+broþor	to give a brother	possession	3
13	acwellan+broþor	to kill a brother	activity	3
14	lufian+broþor	to love a brother	emotion	3
15	asendan+broþor	to send a brother	activity	3
–	other	–	–	30
–	total recurrent	–	–	101

(98) & se Iouis wearð swa swyðe gal þæt he **on**
and the Jovis became so very wicked that he on
his agenre **swyster gewifode**, seo wæs genamod
his own sister married who was named
Iuno,
Juno
'And Jovis became so wicked that he married his own sister, whose name was Juno.' (cowulf,WHom_12:47.1182)

For *broþor* 'brother' the activity verbs listed in Table 43 are much more varied, with *ofslean* 'to kill' in (99) as the most frequent one.

(99) and wiþ Bachidem feaht, þe his **broþor ofsloh**,
and with Bachid fought who his brother killed
'And he fought against Bachid, who killed his brother.' (coaelive,+ALS_[Maccabees]:715.5301)

There is also a verb of emotion *lufian* 'to love' shown in (100), but all examples are about the situation when you actually do not love your brother (and what happens next).

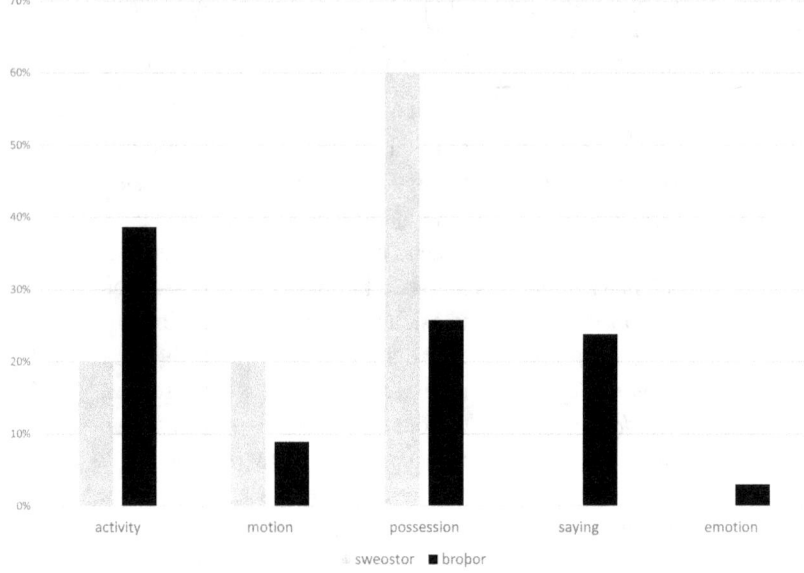

Figure 33 Verbal collocates of *sweostor* 'sister' vs. *broþor* 'brother' as objects in YCOE.

(100) | Se | ðe | ne | **lufað** | his | **broðer** | þone | þe | he | gesihð:
 | this | who | not | loves | his | brother | whom | that | he | sees
 | hu | mæg | he | lufian | God. | þone | ðe | he | ne | gesihð
 | how | may | he | love | God. | whom | that | he | not | sees
 | lichamlice.
 | physically

'If someone does not love his brother, whom he can see, how can he love God, whom he cannot see physically?' (cocathom1,+ACHom_I,_16:309.64.2977)

Figure 33 confirms the patten established in the previous groups: verbs of possession are much more strongly associated with the female terms (60 per cent vs. 27 per cent), though one needs to be cautious when interpreting the graph because of the low number of collocations with *sweostor* 'sister'.

4.2.5 Terms Denoting Women and Men of High Social Status

In the final group, it is impossible to come up with a graph at all since the only recurrent collocation of a woman of higher social status used as a syntactic object is *(to) nunnan gehalgian* 'consecrate a nun', found five times in YCOE and shown in (101).

(101) Þa   berad   mann   þæt wif   þæt   he   hæfde   ær   genumen
      then   seized   man   the woman   that   he   had   before   taken
      butan   þæs   cinges leafe   and   ofer þara   bisceopa
      without the king's permission and   over the   bishops'
      gebodu,   forðon heo wæs   ær   **to   nunnan   gehalgod**.
      command   because she was   before to   nun   consecrated
      'Then they seized the woman who had been taken without the king's permission
      and against the will of the bishops, because she had been a consecrated nun.'
      (cochronC,ChronC_[Rositzke]:901.13.1020)

The pattern is also in use for other official positions one may be ordained to, for example, a bishop or a king as in (102).

(102) and   he   wæs   on   þam   ylcan   geare   **to   cinge   gehalgod**.
      and   he   was   on   the   same   year   to   king   consecreated
      'And the same year he was consecrated king.' (cochronC,ChronC_[Rositzke]:978.1.1174)

Because of higher frequencies, the male-gendered nouns for men of higher social standing are better attested, though not particularly frequent (which shows that the higher your position, the less likely you are to appear as a syntactic object, which is only logical). Table 44 lists the attested patterns. It turns out that the most frequent collocation is *cyning ofslean* 'to kill a king' shown in (103).

(103) &   þone   **cyning   ofslogan**
      and   the   king   killed
      'And (they) killed the king.' (coorosiu,Or_5:4.118.17.2486)

Unlike in the previous categories, the terms denoting women of higher social status are extremely rarely used as grammatical objects. On the one hand, this indicates their more limited involvement in social activities, but, on the other, it might also suggest that such women were not objectified as often as women of lower social status.

4.3 Quantitative Summary

The analysis of verbs collocating with gendered nouns in the role of syntactic subjects was based on 379 phraseological units with female terms and 2,299 units with equivalent male terms. Figure 34 shows the main areas of discrepancy. As can be seen, collocates of male-gendered nouns are much more varied and less dominated by verbs of being (43 per cent for women and (only) 27 per cent for men) and saying (13 per cent vs. 4 per cent respectively), both of which are semantically neutral and not signifying any involvement in social life. The most important difference is visible in the use of activity verbs, which are not only less

Table 44 Verbal collocates of *cyning* 'king', *hlaford* 'lord', *abbod* 'abbot' and *munuc* 'monk' as objects (> 6) in YCOE

Number	Lemma	Translation	Pattern	Σ
1	ofslean+cyning	to kill a king	activity	39
2	gehalgian+to+cyning	to consecrate (as) king	activity	18
3	habban+cyning	to have a king	possession	15
4	gecyþan+cyning	to inform a king	saying	11
5	geceosan+cyning	to choose a king	activity	10
6	secgan+cyning	to tell a king	saying	9
7	secgan+hlaford	to tell a lord	saying	8
8	slean+cyning	to kill a king	activity	7
9	onfon+cyning	to take a king	possession	7
10	gesecan+cyning	to seek a king	activity	7
11	foresprecan+cyning	to promise to a king	commitment	7
12	sendan+cyning	to send a king	activity	6
13	brengan+cyning	to bring to a king	possession	6
14	underfon+cyning	to take a king	possession	6
15	habban+hlaford	to have a lord	possession	6
16	þeowian+hlaford	to serve a lord	activity	6
–	other	–	–	162
–	total recurrent	–	–	330

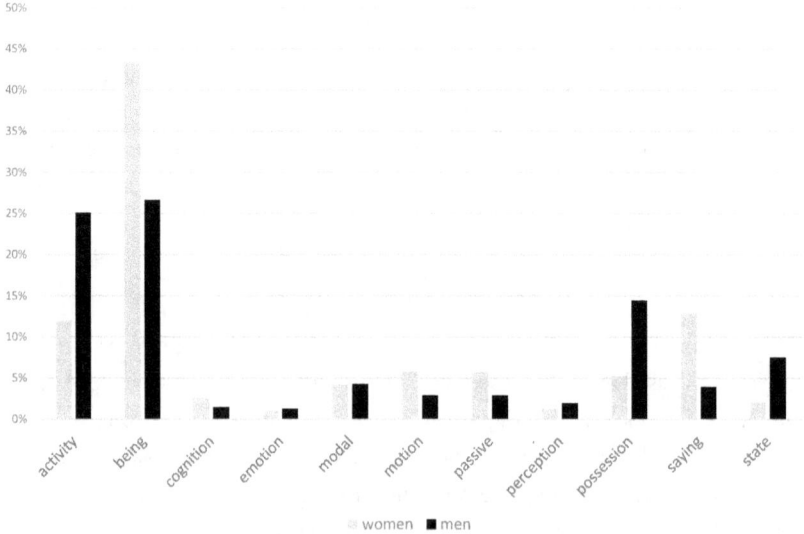

Figure 34 Verbal collocates of all the gendered nouns as subjects: Summary.

frequent in the case of female-gendered subjects (12 per cent vs. 25 per cent), but also much less diverse and centred around marriage and childbearing, as shown in Section 4.1. Another important difference concerns verbs of possession, which co-occur with female subjects in only 5 per cent of the dataset, with the equvalent result for males at 14 per cent. The differences are statistically significant (X2 (4, N = 2678) = 128.4473, p < 0.00001).[14] The results confirm a much less diverse array of activities available for women in the early Middle Ages and the primary role of women as mothers and housewives.

As far as collocations with gendered nouns as objects are concerned, the analysis takes into account 264 units with female terms and 840 units with male terms. Figure 35 presents the data for all of the analysed nouns combined, and it is quite clear that verbs of possession are the main point of divergence here, with as much as 62 per cent of the dataset for female-gendered nouns covered by this category and with only 23 per cent of the male-gendered nouns as the equivalent result (most of which are collocations of *sunu* 'son', relating to a younger and therefore less socially prestigious male). A less conspicuous but equally interesting difference which only comes to light when all of the collocations are

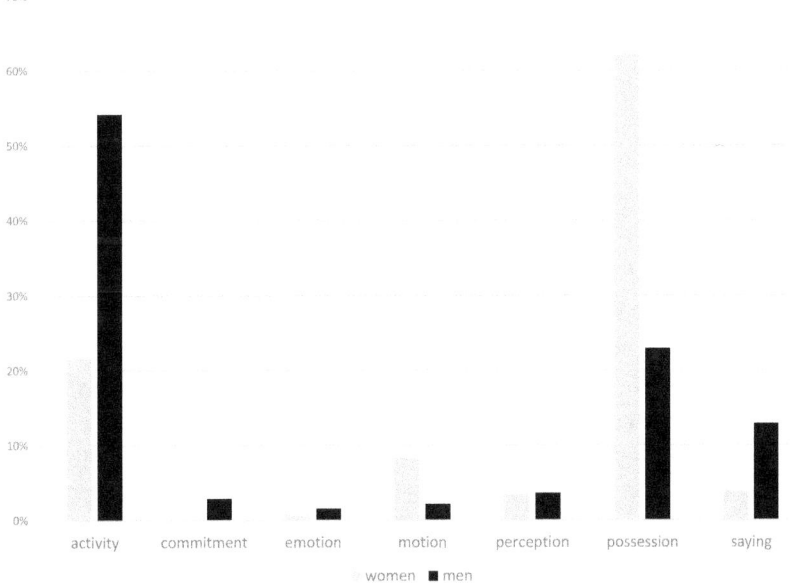

Figure 35 Verbal collocates of all the gendered nouns as objects: Summary.

---

[14] In the statistical analysis we have only taken into account verbs of being, possession, activity and saying as separate categories, collapsing all the remaining data into 'other', since most of the available online chi-square calculators allow for the analysis of the maximum of five categories. Thus, only the most frequent ones could be selected.

inspected together is visible for verbs of saying: as can be seen, men are relatively often the indirect objects of reporting structures (13 per cent), while women are passive interlocutors much less often (4 per cent).

Obviously, activity verbs are again a huge area of difference, with 54 per cent of the male dataset classified as such (let us recall that a big part of these examples are verbs of killing), and only 22 per cent of female-gendered nouns appearing in this category. Statistics confirms the significance of this difference (X^2 (3, N = 1104) = 158.5192, p < 0.00001).[15] The results provide a clear linguistic confirmation of the dominance of men in Anglo-Saxon society and the secondary position of women who were 'owned' by their fathers and husbands.

Conclusions

The linguistic data analysed in this study clearly indicate a disparity between the representations of women and men in late Old English society. They are invariably disproportionate in favour of the male gender: texts forming the corpus describe men as superior owners, engaged in productive activities in the public domain, while women are portrayed mostly in terms of property and as passive vessels. Given the interconnection between language and the reality it depicts, such a polarisation must be seen as a reflection of the actual divide between the female and the male in late Anglo-Saxon England. Although this state of play is not particularly surprising, as it corresponds to the data documented in historical sources, it incontrovertibly demonstrates that gender-based favouritism was plainly visible on the level of Old English public discourse.

The results presented in Sections 3 and 4 repeatedly and consistently substantiate that the ways in which women and men are seen through the language of Old English prose are drastically different. In the analysed collocations, Anglo-Saxon women are commonly depicted in the context of their physicality: inasmuch as their bodies are often directly mentioned, they are perceived through such factors as age, sexual attractiveness and ability to bear children. They are not shown as important agents of social life: the women terms rarely collocate with activity verbs, and even if they do, it is usually in connection with marriage and childbearing. Their relation to men is clearly subordinate: the woman is usually presented not as the owner of property, but as property itself, and she may be owned and transferred between men (usually from a father to a husband). The unprivileged position of the female gender is also implied

---

[15] In the statistical analysis we have only taken into account verbs of possession, activity and saying as separate categories, collapsing all the remaining data into 'other' because of their equally low frequency.

through the discursive position of women and men: although the representatives of both genders are described as speaking equally often, women are rarely spoken to, as if they did not deserve the same interlocutor status as men.

The linguistic image of Anglo-Saxon men, in contrast, is that of agents involved in social life: they perform a wide range of various activities, which are notably not related to household and family. Men are not perceived in terms of their physicality; instead, the male terms often collocate with words signifying the position of power (in all groups with the exception of male children, which only reinforces the proposition that once a man achieves maturity, he attains a dominant social status). Unlike women, men in Anglo-Saxon England are linguistically depicted as property owners, and they are as a rule not objectified. They are much more frequently described with positive terms, often relating to the religious sphere.

The juxtaposition of members of different genders also confirms male domination in Anglo-Saxon society. Whenever a female term is conjoined with a noun referring to a male, the latter always comes first, which emphasises the superiority of men: a man is prioritised over a woman, a father over a mother, a son over a daughter. While the corpus abounds in examples of pairs of two male terms, it does not noticeably feature pairs of two women, which suggests that the image of all-female social units was not particularly promoted by Old English texts. Additionally, the very frequency of some collocations is meaningful: the fact that some word groups are so disproportionately represented (e.g. the paucity of data concerning collocations featuring female equivalents of 'brother' or 'son') clearly indicates the privileged position of the male gender. Finally, it is interesting that the female terms from the category comprising women of higher social status can form collocations similar to the patterns displayed in all male term categories. This demonstrates that in late Anglo-Saxon society it was necessary for a woman to maintain a position of a queen, an aristocrat or an abbess to enjoy a linguistic image of a standing which corresponded to that of a man.

Certainly, an important caveat of this Element is that the texts gathered in the corpus analysed are all highly biased. The literate Anglo-Saxon elite responsible for the production of Old English written records consisted solely of middle-aged, well-educated males, mostly members of the clergy. Thus the linguistic image of women in Old English texts is filtered through the minds of a small (though highly influential) portion of Anglo-Saxon society. Because of this textual limitation, we have no access to the way in which all speakers of Old English used collocations based on gendered nouns and we can only draw conclusions from the material at our disposal. It is also crucial to remember that the linguistic representations created by the texts from the corpus are not only the images of Anglo-Saxon women (and men) that the authors themselves experienced, but also the images that they *would like to experience*. Language is not only a tool for describing reality, but also an instrument of power, and, consequently, we must consider the linguistic representations of women (and men) established in this study as not only descriptive, but also prescriptive.

Furthermore, neither the sources of the linguistic representation of women in Anglo-Saxon society nor its long-term effects can be properly assessed without considering the context of the Christian religion. As we have mentioned before, the majority of texts analysed in this study are of ecclesiastical origins, being mostly sermons and lives of saints. Such texts were significant elements of male power discourse designed and maintained by the church: a clear objective of both these genres was to provide society with moral parameters and patterns of desirable behaviour. In this context it becomes of crucial importance that the textual evidence provided by our analysis agrees with Hollis's (1992) hypothesis about the downgrading influence of Roman Christianity on the position of women in Anglo-Saxon society. For instance, frequent references to women in terms of their corporality align with Hollis's claim that 'the distinctively "other" identity the church postulated for women ... chiefly consisted in the carnal frailty they inherited from Eve' (Hollis, 1992: 11). Such a masculinist or even misogynistic outlook has already been noted by the feminist critique of the Christian religious and ideological doctrine: for instance, Kristeva (1986) sees the roots of female deprecation and discrimination in the biblical story of Eve and the serpent: the myth establishes the woman as a source of corruption (often equated with the body), and the resultant socio-political system requires that women 'are excluded from knowledge and power' (Kristeva, 1986: 143). As Irigaray (1993) emphatically puts it: 'The positive connotation of the masculine ... derives from the time of the establishment of patriarchal and phallocratic power, notably by men's appropriation of the divine. ... [M]an becomes God by giving himself an invisible father, a father language. Man becomes God as the Word, then as the Word made flesh' (Irigaray, 1993: 86).

The dichotomy between the linguistic representation of men and women determined in this Element clearly privileges one side over the other – active over passive, subject over object, culture over nature, spirit over body – following a Platonic Christian pattern. If we assume that language indeed determines, or at least strongly affects, one's thinking and perception, then we must acknowledge that male-oriented language used in England between the ninth century and the eleventh century was one of the factors responsible for later alienation and discrimination of women, shaping the perception of gender roles in England in the following centuries. If we agree with Cameron that 'representations of language and gender are part of the social apparatus which legitimizes and so helps to maintain gender distinctions and hierarchies' (Cameron, 2014: 285), then we should claim that late Anglo-Saxon gender representations served their purpose really effectively.

References

Bennett, H. T. (1994). Exile and the Semiosis of Gender in Old English Elegies. In B. J. Harwood and G. R. Overing, eds., *Class and Gender in Early English Literature*. Bloomington: Indiana University Press, pp. 43–58.

Bennett, H. T., Lees, C. A. & Overing, G. R. (1990). Anglo Saxon Studies: Gender and Power. Feminism in Old English Studies. *Medieval Feminist Newsletter*, 10, 15–24.

Bennett, J. M. (1988). Public Power and Authority in the Medieval English Countryside. In M. Erler and M. Kowaleski, eds., *Women and Power in the Middle Ages*. Athens: University of Georgia Press, pp. 18–36.

Blakar, R. M. (1977). *Språk er makt [Language Is Power]*. Oslo: Pax.

Bucholtz, M. (2014). The Feminist Foundations of Language, Gender, and Sexuality Research. In S. Ehrlich, M. Meyerhoff and J. Holmes, eds., *The Handbook of Language, Gender, and Sexuality*, 2nd ed. London: Wiley Blackwell, pp. 23–47.

Cameron, D. (1992). *Feminism and Linguistic Theory*, 2nd ed. Basingstoke: Macmillan.

Cameron, D. (2014). Gender and Language Ideologies. In S. Ehrlich, M. Meyerhoff and J. Holmes, eds., *The Handbook of Language, Gender, and Sexuality*, 2nd ed. London: Wiley Blackwell, pp. 281–296.

Chance, J. (1986). *Woman as Hero in Old English Literature*. Syracuse, NY: Syracuse University Press.

Chance, J. (2007). *The Literary Subversions of Medieval Women*. New York: Palgrave Macmillan.

Cichosz, A., Pęzik, P., Grabski, M. Adamczyk, M., Rybińska, P. & Ostrowska, A. (2021). The VARIOE online morphological dictionary for YCOE. University of Lodz. varioe.pelcra.pl/morph.

Cixous, H. (1976). The Laugh of the Medusa, trans. K. Cohen and P. Cohen. *Signs*, 1(4), 875–893.

Damico, H. (1984). Beowulf's *Wealhtheow and the Valkyrie Tradition*. Madison: University of Wisconsin Press.

Damico, H. (2015). Beowulf *and the Grendel-kin: Politics & Poetry in Eleventh-Century England*. Morgantown: West Virginia University Press.

Desmond, M. (1990). The Voice of Exile: Feminist Literary History and the Anonymous Anglo-Saxon Elegy. *Critical Inquiry*, 16(4), 572–590.

Etymonline. woman n. www.etymonline.com.

Fee, C. (1996). *Beag & Beaghroden*: Women, Treasure and the Language of Social Structure in *Beowulf. Neuphilologische Mitteilungen*, 97(3), 285–294.

Fell, C. (1986). *Women in Anglo-Saxon England*, 2nd ed. Oxford: Basil Blackwell.

Fishman, P. (1983). Interaction: The Work Women Do. In B. Thorne, C. Kramarae and N. Henley, eds., *Language, Gender, and Society*. Rowley, MA: Newbury House, pp. 89–102.

Fox, A. (2000). *Oral and Literate Culture in England, 1500–1700*. Oxford: Oxford University Press.

García Meseguer, Á. (1977). *Lenguaje y discriminacion sexual* [*Language and Sex Discrimination*]. Madrid: Editorial Cuadernos para el Dialogo, S. A. Edicusa.

Goldberg, A. E. & Lee, C. (2021). Accessibility and Historical Change: An Emergent Cluster Led Uncles and Aunts to Become Aunts and Uncles. *Frontiers in Psychology*, 12, 1–19.

Greenfield, S. B. (1965). *A Critical History of Old English Literature*, New York University Press, 1965.

Guentherodt, I., Hellinger, M., Pusch, L. & Troemel-Ploetz, S. (1980). Richtlinien zuer Vermeidung sexistischen Sprachgebrauchs [Guidelines for the Elimination of Sexist Language Use]. *Linguistische Berichte*, 69, 15–21.

Harris, R. (2014). The Women of *Beowulf*: Power and Duty in Anglo-Saxon Society. *The Paper Shell Review*. https://english.umd.edu/research-innovation/journals/paper-shell-review/paper-shell-review-spring-2014/women-beowulf-power.

Hendricks, C. & Oliver, K. (1999). Introduction: How to Do (Feminist) Things with Words. In K. Oliver and C. Hendricks, eds., *Language and Liberation: Feminism, Philosophy, and Language*. Albany: State University of New York Press, pp. 1–39.

Hogg, R. (2006). Old English Dialectology. In A. van Kemenade and B. Los, eds., *The Handbook of the History of English*. Oxford: Blackwell, pp. 395–416.

Hollis, S. (1992). *Anglo-Saxon Women and the Church: Sharing a Common Fate*. Rochester, NY: Boydell Press.

Irigaray, L. (1985). *This Sex Which Is Not One*, trans. C. Porter and C. Burke. Ithaca, NY: Cornell University Press.

Irigaray, L. (1993). *Je, Tu, Nous: Toward a Culture of Difference*, trans. A. Martin. New York: Routledge.

Karwatowska, M. & Szpyra-Kozłowska, J. (2005). *Lingwistyka płci: ona i on w języku polskim* [*The Linguistics of Gender: She and He in Polish*]. Wydawnictwo UMCS: Lublin.

Key, M. R. (1975). *Male/Female Language*. Metuchen, NJ: Scarecrow Press.

Klinck, A. L. (1982). Anglo-Saxon Women and the Law. *Journal of Medieval History*, 8(2), 107–121.

Kotek, H., Dockum, R., Babinski, S. & Geissler, C. (2020). Gender Bias and Stereotypes in Linguistic Example Sentences. *Language*, 97(4), 653–677.

Kristeva, J. (1986). *The Kristeva Reader*, ed. T. Moi, trans. L. S. Roudiez and S. Hand. New York: Columbia University Press.

Lacan, J. (2006). *Écrits*, trans. B. Fink. New York: W. W. Norton & Company.

Lakoff, R. (1975). *Language and Woman's Place*. New York: Harper and Row.

Lee, C. (2023). Embroidered Narratives. In R. Norris, R. Stephenson and R. R. Trilling, eds., *Feminist Approaches to Early Medieval English Studies*. Amsterdam: Amsterdam University Press, pp. 53–82.

Lees, C. A. (1997). At a Crossroads: Old English and Feminist Criticism. In K. O'Brien O-Keeffe, ed., *Reading Old English Texts*. Cambridge: Cambridge University Press, pp. 146–169.

Leyser, H. (1995). *Medieval Women: A Social History of Women in England, 450–1500*, New York: St. Martin's Press.

Marco, M. J. L. (1997). Linguistic Choices for the Representation of Women in Discourse. *Bells: Barcelona English Language and Literature Studies*, 8, 247–259.

Nevalainen, T. & Raumolin-Brunberg, H. (2003). *Historical Sociolinguistics: Language Change in Tudor and Stuart England*, London: Routledge.

Norris, R., Stephenson, R. & Trilling, R. R. (2023). Introduction. In R. Norris, R. Stephenson and R. R. Trilling, eds., *Feminist Approaches to Early Medieval English Studies*. Amsterdam: Amsterdam University Press, pp. 9–25.

Overing, G. R. (1990). *Language, Sign, and Gender in* Beowulf, Carbondale: Southern Illinois University Press.

Oxford English Dictionary. 'man, n.1 (and int.)'. Oxford University Press. www.oed.com.

Pauwels, A. (2005). Linguistic Sexism and Feminist Linguistic Activism. In J. Holmes and M. Meyerhoff, eds., *The Handbook of Language and Gender*. Oxford: Blackwell, pp. 550–570.

Pęzik, P. & Cichosz, A. (2021). The VARIOE Online Dictionary of Old English Collocations. University of Lodz. varioe.pelcra.pl/collocations.

Phillips, B. S. (1990). Nicknames and Sex Role Stereotypes. *Sex Roles*, 23, 281–289.

Pintzuk, Susan & Plug, L. (2001). The York–Helsinki Parsed Corpus of Old English Poetry. Department of Linguistics, University of York. Oxford Text Archive. www-users.york.ac.uk/~lang18/pcorpus.html.

Roberts, J. & Kay, C. with L. Grundy. (2000). *A Thesaurus of Old English*, 2nd ed. King's College London Medieval Studies XI. Amsterdam: Rodopi.

Schulz, M. (1975). *The Semantic Derogation of Woman*. New York: Thorne and Henley.

Spender, D. (1980). *Man Made Language*. London: Routledge & Kegan Paul.

Stenton, D. (1957). *The English Woman in History* London: George Allen and Unwin.

Taylor, A., Warner, A., Pintzuk, S. & Beths, F. (2003). The York–Toronto–Helsinki Parsed Corpus of Old English Prose (YCOE). Department of Linguistics, University of York. Oxford Text Archive (www-users.york.ac.uk/~lang22/YcoeHome1.htm).

Uri, H. (2018). *Hvem sa hva? [Who Said What?]*. Oslo: Gyldendal.

Weatherall, A. (2002). *Gender, Language and Discourse*. New York: Routledge.

Wormald, C. P. (1977). The Uses of Literacy in Anglo-Saxon England and Its Neighbours. *Transactions of the Royal Historical Society*, 27, 95–114.

Yaguello, M. (1978). *Les mots et les femmes [Words and Women]*. Paris: Payot.

Acknowledgments

This book was developed as part of the project entitled *The linguistic image of woman in Old English Prose* (IDUB B2311313000191.07) financed by the University of Lodz.

Cambridge Elements

Language, Gender and Sexuality

Helen Sauntson
York St John University

Helen Sauntson is Professor of English Language and Linguistics at York St John University, UK. Her research areas are language in education and language, gender and sexuality. She is co-editor of *The Palgrave Studies in Language, Gender and Sexuality* book series, and she sits on the editorial boards of the journals *Gender and Language* and the *Journal of Language and Sexuality*. Within her institution, Helen is Director of the Centre for Language and Social Justice Research.

Editorial Board
Lilian Lem Atanga, *The University of Bamenda*
Eva Nossem, *Saarland University*
Joshua M. Paiz, *The George Washington University*
M. Agnes Kang, *University of Hong Kong*

About the Series
Cambridge Elements in Language, Gender and Sexuality highlights the role of language in understanding issues, identities and relationships in relation to multiple genders and sexualities. The series provides a comprehensive home for key topics in the field which readers can consult for up-to-date coverage and the latest developments.

Cambridge Elements

Language, Gender and Sexuality

Elements in the Series

The Language of Gender-Based Separatism
Veronika Koller, Alexandra Krendel and Jessica Aiston

Queering Sexual Health Translation Pedagogy
Piero Toto

Legal Categorization of 'Transgender': An Analysis of Statutory Interpretation of 'Sex', 'Man', and 'Woman' in Transgender Jurisprudence
Kimberly Tao

LGBTQ+ and Feminist Digital Activism: A Linguistic Perspective
Angela Zottola

Feminism, Corpus-assisted Research and Language Inclusivity
Federica Formato

Queering Language Revitalisation: Navigating Identity and Inclusion among Queer Speakers of Minority Languages
John Walsh, Michael Hornsby, Eva J. Daussà, Renée Pera-Ros, Samuel Parker, Jonathan Morris and Holly R. Cashman

Pride in Asia: Negotiating Ideologies, Localness, and Alternative Futures
Benedict J. L. Rowlett, Pavadee Saisuwan, Christian Go,
Li-Chi Chen and Mie Hiramoto

Language, Gender and Pregnancy Loss
Beth Malory

Discourse and Queer Sinophone Male Identities: A Western Immigrant Perspective
Phil Freestone

Linguistic Representations of Women in Old English Prose: A Corpus-Based Phraseological Study
Anna Cichosz and Tomasz Dobrogoszcz

A full series listing is available at: www.cambridge.org/ELGS

For EU product safety concerns, contact us at Calle de José Abascal, 56–1°, 28003 Madrid, Spain or eugpsr@cambridge.org.

www.ingramcontent.com/pod-product-compliance
Lightning Source LLC
LaVergne TN
LVHW011847060526
838200LV00054B/4218